The ULT.

# TRAVEL
# WRITING
# TRAVEL
# AGENTS

### SELL MORE TRAVEL
### BY WRITING ABOUT IT

## Stephen Crowhurst, CTC

TRAVEL WRITING TRAVEL AGENTS
SELL MORE TRAVEL
BY WRITING ABOUT IT

ISBN-13: 978-1717580474
ISBN-10: 1717580475

Cover: Stephen Crowhurst
Illustrations by Stephen Crowhurst.

Published by Stephen Crowhurst through CreateSpace

Font: Garamond 12.5

Printed in the United States of America

# TRAVEL WRITING
# TRAVEL AGENTS

## How to Write About and Profit
## From Your Travel Experiences

"Many travellers are already familiar with your destination expertise. Now take this to the next level and post your seasoned travel advice and experience-based observations online or in print. Maximize the knowledge impact you have on your current client base and attract new clients looking for refreshing ideas and enthusiasm."

*Steve Gillick, Gillick's World*

# Dedications

This book is dedicated to the following people:

### Anthony Dalton, FRGS, FRCGS
Adventurer, speaker, photographer and author.
Anthony has encouraged me over the years to write
not only marketing books, but also novels.
A great friend and teacher.
www.anthonydalton.net

### Arthur Proudfoot (deceased)
A former contributor to Canadian Travel Press.
In 1983, Arthur walked into my office, placed an old Kaypro
computer on my desk saying, "It's about time, sonny!"
That was my first computer and launched my writing career.

### Scott Barker, Big Bark Graphics
It was Scott who called me up and said,
"I wanna publish that!" referring to my 400-page,
marketing idea book for travel agents – and he did.
www.bigbarkgraphics.com

### Steve Gillick, Gillick's World
One of the best travel writers in the world.
Well-travelled. Humourous. A Japanophile,
trainer, traveller, teacher, writer, speaker and
photographer – Steve is the traveller's traveller.
He respects and appreciates what makes
this world so exciting to travel.
www.gillicksworld.ca

# TABLE OF CONTENTS

## BONUS PAGES

HOW TO PUBLISH YOUR TRAVEL BOOK ON AMAZON.COM

Not long now and you will be
on your way to the
ULTIMATE
DUAL CAREER
in the entire travel & tourism industry.

Hi, thanks for purchasing Travel Writing Travel Agents.

I hope you can find the time to enjoy the ultimate dual career as a travel writing seller of travel. The two go together so well – and besides, you are already in the travel business. You are halfway there! Bonus!

This book is NOT about how to write. For that, you will need to study elsewhere. This book IS about how to use your writing skills to sell more travel and grow your travel writing/travel selling career.

Okay, time to follow the arrow. Enjoy.

Steve Crowhurst, CTC
www.sellingtravel.net

# INTRODUCTION: WRITING TO GROW YOUR SALES

The focus of this book is the same for all my publications, and that is: to help you, the travel agent, grow your sales. In my world, that's called New Business Generation, or NBG. Attracting new business to your agency is what agents tell me is their number one challenge. The second, number one challenge is: closing the sale before the prospect walks and books online.

For those of you who Love to Travel and Long to Write, this book is for you. It comes with the mandate, however, that you write to showcase your travels and expertise and promote your travel services to sell more travel. Here's the thing: when you publish a book, you somehow elevate your status. It's true. Your travel writing will win you radio and TV interviews, invitations to join media trips and more.

The key to growing your travel sales by writing about your travel experiences is to write to your audience. Showcase your passion for a type of travel or a particular destination. Your fame will grow once you learn how to market what you have written.

It is a well-known fact that almost everyone wants to write a book. It is a worthy cause. Starting and finishing can be a year apart. For most people who attempt to write a book, they dry up after the first one thousand words. It ain't easy, that's for sure.

If you stick with it, writing a page a day, for instance, you will finish that travel guide or the romance novel set in Tuscany. You have the world ahead of you. Perhaps you write now to grow your sales, and eventually, you write an award-winning novel. Who knows? Starting is the key.

Today, you can self-publish using the free CreateSpace tools offered by Amazon. You will need an editor to edit your writing and a graphic artist to produce your cover – unless you can DIY it.

# HOW IT ALL STARTED FOR ME

My travel writing career started when I was a teenager sending postcards to Mum and Dad as I travelled with my school's outward bound program. The postcards home continued as a teenager hitchhiking around my native United Kingdom. After that, I upgraded to writing letters as I sailed around the world with a lot more to write home about.

The best thing about my writing home was that Mum, who was an avid scribe herself (she wrote to my Dad every day for the five years he was a POW during WW2), had kept every letter and postcard I'd ever sent home. Even as I write this book, my box of cards and letters home, dating from 1962 – 1969, are right beside me.

My father also loved to write, and just as Mum had written to him, so my Dad wrote to me while I was at sea and he continued writing to me after I had left the UK to emigrate to Canada in 1970. We were a writing kind of family.

My official travel writing career started when I wrote for Tim Baxter (Baxter Publishing) who was publishing the PATA Americas Magazine in 1987. In 2001, I began to write a monthly column for CT Canadian Traveller magazine.

I went on to publish my own e-magazines, specifically Selling Travel and IC Travel Agent. Both can be still read on Issuu.com.

## My New Writing Adventure and Yours Too!

I mentioned that your writing could take you from writing articles to writing a travel guide, to writing a novel. I suggested a novel because I have just written and published one myself, so I know it can be done.

The focus of this book is travel writing, but, what if you did have an excellent idea for a romance novel set in your favourite location. A place you know so well. The story could pop into your head while lounging on the beach, walking in the woods, having a gourmet meal somewhere or writing your next post on your blog. What if?

My new writing adventure has turned out two novels so far and based on a theme and a passion of mine since I was a teenager – Japan and historical events that involve ninja, samurai and swords. Here are the covers of my recent publications. Imagine that these are YOUR novels. People read them. Love them. They want to travel "there." They book with you. Nice!

Be sure to visit www.sellingtravel.net for my new eGuides.
My novels can be discovered here: www.stephencrowhurst.com

# WHAT IS A TRAVEL WRITER AND WHY BE ONE?

Most travel writers just write about their own travels. They are hooked on travelling, and they love to write. Alternatively, they love to write and want to finance their next trip. The challenge for the typical travel writer is their take-home pay. They do not make very much money each month – or so the survey says. Then, of course, there's always the super travel writer who makes that magic million, give or take a cent.

The difference between you and the typical travel writer is that you are a travel agent and you already generate income from your day job which could and should finance your travel writing. You have connections, you have access to FAM trips and you can, if you own the agency, take off travelling as and when you desire.

This gentleman is my buddy Thomas Cook. Yes, the one and only. I used to work for the company and took an interest in this man and his son. He was a printer by trade and had those skills when he opened his tour and travel business. He created, he travelled, he wrote guide books and he built an empire. Any travel agent and travel writer worth their words should read the biography of this man and his son, Mason Cook.

If you work for a travel agency as an employee, then you write about your past travels and add to your articles each year when you take a vacation or FAM. If you are home-based and work as an independent contractor, then the dual career of travel agent/travel writer is waiting for you on your terms.

Just so we have it right, let's source a definition for a travel writer. Who are they? What do they do?

Look for the book "Romantic Journey"

Following is a brief definition of travel writing found on Wikipedia:

Travel writing is a genre that has, as its focus, accounts of real or imaginary places. The genre encompasses a number of styles that may range from the documentary to the evocative, from literary to journalistic, and from the humorous to the serious. Travel writing is often associated with tourism and includes works of an ephemeral nature such as guidebooks and reviews, with the intent being to educate the reader about the destination, provide helpful advice for those visiting the destination, and inspire readers to travel to the destination. Effective travel writing should allow readers a vivid recollection of the area/areas being described in a way that is useful and entertaining. Travel writing of various degrees of quality may be found on websites, in magazines and in books. Travel writing has also been produced by other types of travellers, such as military officers, missionaries, explorers, scientists, pilgrims, and migrants.

http://en.wikipedia.org/wiki/Travel_writer#Travel_writing

Being a travel agent, selling travel and then writing about travel is to build a dual career based on a solid business footing. Plus, as mentioned, you have access to more resources than your average travel writer. This access to agency resources is why the concept of you building a travel writing career makes sense. Somewhere down the road, you may have to choose one path over the other – or enjoy the benefits of both careers.

It is okay to think about that dual career and do a little daydreaming, too. However, if you love to travel and long to write, perhaps it is time to make a move, or at least investigate your next step.

Remember, you do not have to quit being a travel agent. Being a travel agent is your route to being a travel writer and travel writing will increase your travel sales. It's a perfect match.

# TRAVEL & WRITING – A DUAL CAREER

You CAN have your cake and eat it too! Yes, you can. Are you single and ready to trot the globe? Are you married with a family? Would anyone mind if you took off for about, well, let's see, let's go for about ten months? Could you be gone more than usual? Would you take your family with you and write as you go? You could. All the available technology makes it possible.

You could, if you were ready to commit, sign up with BootsnAll and be prepared to post your first travel blog feature. At BootsnAll you will find so much information on how to become a great writer, plus how BootsnAll might factor into your life and you into theirs.

---

Here's the introduction for prospective BootsnAll writers. It's taken from their website. Visit their website for the rest of the information.

## Write for BootsnAll! Current Writing Opportunities:

We are accepting article pitches again, but we are looking for very specific ideas. Please make sure that before you pitch any ideas that you take a look at the various opportunities we offer below (what we are looking for differs based on the writing program). It's also a good idea to read through our **Indie Travel Manifesto** to see if your story seems like a good fit. If the story you had in mind doesn't reflect at least one (and preferably more) tenets of the Manifesto, then BootsnAll isn't the right forum

<u>http://writers.bootsnall.com/platform</u>

---

You might want to check with your owner, manager or host head office and ask if they need a travel writer. Chances are you could become the official writer of the agency blog or the publisher of the agency e-magazine. What a great place to start your travel writing career and still earn a salary from selling travel. Start your career from inside the agency where you work or host agency/group you are affiliated with.

# RESEARCHING AND DUE DILIGENCE

Travel and writing sound like a match made in heaven. I know you are excited and want to get on the road, get in the air, climb that mountain and take another cruise. However, there's more to writing about travel than just tapping a keyboard. You will need to follow someone's advice, and you will need to dig a little deeper in regarding how your new career will affect your current lifestyle and current source of revenue.

To help you dig a little deeper let me introduce you to two websites that you should subscribe to and when the timing is right, sign up for the workshops and training programs that appeal to you.

Great Escape Publishing offers you both sides of the travel coin: travel writing and travel photography. If a writer's life is not for you, perhaps the photography side of travel is. Either way you can develop a dual career with your selling travel day job being the hub.

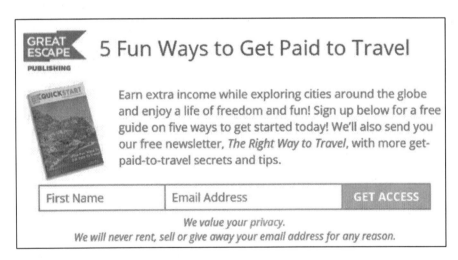

Finding the time to travel and write, will be your challenge. It is important, when you make your move into travel writing, that you do so, knowing how much time you can invest. If you work for someone else, then your life is decided for you. Perhaps you can negotiate your working /travelling /writing time allotment.

Let's continue on with your research and education, and introduce you to a few more websites and then we'll move on to how you can profit from your existing and future travel experiences.

Here's my copy of the QuickStart guide that is free to download from Great Escape Publishing. The 46-page guide offers you excellent information and you'll be chomping at the bit to get out there to gather content for your travel articles. You can download your copy of Quickstart by visiting this link: https://www.greatescapepublishing.com/

Two more books for you to check out. The Writer's Market is for all writers, not just travel writers. The Lonely Planet guide, How To Be A Travel Writer, is dedicated as the title suggests.

The Lonely Planet book will help you develop your writing style. Then you can plan which style would be compatible with the magazines you select from the Writer's Market book.

## Women Travel Writers and Adventurers

Travel writing is open to everyone. As you research and explore those who have gone before you, you will notice that it was a man's world until recently. Today, more and more women are travelling the globe and writing about their experiences. Not only that, the travel agency community is populated by women to the tune of around 85%. So look for travel books written by women and find the inspiration to continue with your travel writing dream.

In the 1800's it was, as I say, a man's world and it was generally a man's place to take off on a Grand Tour of at least Europe. Known then as the Grand Tour, designed by Thomas Cook & Son. Eventually, men and women, husbands and wives journeyed together in full Victorian dress. No flip-flops or ball caps allowed back then – however cocaine and opium were fine! Be sure to read the writings of both male and female travel writers. I'll stress the fact that travelogues written by men are a dime a dozen. The books written by women are hard to track down, and so I urge you to explore the two links below where you can find more than a few fascinating and inspiring reads.

When you put yourself back in time, reading the adventures of Freya Stark and others like her, you will be amazed at how they managed to travel without a male escort. You could fast forward to someone like Katherine Hepburn who was ahead of her time and didn't bother checking in for male approval. She wore the pants, and that was it. Same and similar traits seem to run within the DNA of Victorian women seeking their own adventures. They were women of means and had the money to do what they wanted to do. There are accounts of women who were not well off and still managed to fulfill their travel passions. Some even captained ships – merchant and pirate!

http://www.shakariconnection.com/women-traveller-books.html
http://www.longitudebooks.com/

# MEDIA PRESS TRIPS

When you look for media trips, your best connections would be tourism boards and tourism offices of the destinations you wish to visit. On their official destination website, look for a heading that reads Press Trip Policy or similar wording.

My purpose here is to inform you of the level and type of information you will be asked to submit before being accepted on a media/press trip. Mostly the tourism office will want to know about your readership and how you are going to promote their destination once your return to your agency. They'll want a return on their media trip investment which could translate into three or more published articles within a specific time frame.

As a travel agent, you will have access to your existing client list, and this should be mentioned in your submission. You may not yet be writing for a well-known consumer travel magazine, however, you should state the fact that your article will reach and be read by several hundred to several thousand travellers. If you start now, writing and publishing an agency newsletter, e-magazine or a travel blog, you will build a sizable readership that you can promote when you submit your name for a press trip.

Most travel writers contribute to a well-known travel magazine or newspaper with whom they have built a working relationship. You could be ahead of the game if you market yourself as I am suggesting: listing yourself as a ***travel writing travel agent*** with a dedicated travel clientele and readership.

The killer phrase here is this: ***not only will you write about the destination, you will also sell the destination.*** This is important. It's a game changer. It means you will encourage your clients to visit the destination featured during the media trip. That is something the generic travel writer cannot and does not do. The tourism board hosting the media trip will receive more bang for their buck when they accept you on their trip.

# PROFITING FROM YOUR TRAVEL EXPERIENCES

"One day I'm going to write a book." Everyone wants to write a book. How many times have you heard that one? You have probably said it to yourself. Truth be told – it ain't that easy. On the other hand, it's not that difficult either. All you need is a good story, a few thousand words, a terrific opening line, a fantastic spellbinding ending and 100% commitment to finish it. Let's leave the book writing for the moment and concentrate on writing a one-page article.

As an author of a bestselling novel crafts their story, you must craft your one-page travel article. The fact that you have visited Hawaii or Jamaica twenty times will not make for adventurous reading, but it might make for a great guidebook. Having written over 425 magazine articles myself, all one or two pagers, I can tell you it is a tough haul to keep each new article fresh. In your case, you will be travelling as often as you can or drawing on your past travels.

Writing can and will boost your profile in the local marketplace. If an editor tells you to take a hike, it doesn't really matter. With current technology, you can publish anything you want, when you want and to whom you want. All you need is the outlet and the audience, and you have both.

## Check Your Credentials

You will need to build credibility and be able to show your travel scars to prove you actually stood there, walked there and took that shot. You'll need stories to tell. One place to start is to make notes about what you have done, where you've been and build a profile for yourself. Every step, every mile and every place visited is now something you record along with those selfies.

Here is an excellent place to start recalling where you have been and when. TripAdvisor and TravelPod offer a create-your-own-map app. It's a great way to capture your travels. It's easy and fast to do.

Here's my Travel Map. Yours would look like this, too. The map is interactive, and when finished you can copy and paste a link to embed your map into your website. Screen print your map and add it to media trip submission. This map does not record cruise routes, so you could screen capture the map, import it into your graphics program and draw in the routes of the cruises you have taken.

Click to the TripAdvisor Travel Map and start checking off the places you've visited. They scroll up on the right-hand side of the map. Once you've exhausted the places they list, you can type in additional cities you have visited to continue building your map. Once your map is complete, record the numeric details and add them to your profile. Start here: https://www.tripadvisor.com/TravelMapHome

Here's a map of my ocean-going voyages. You should create a similar map and attach it to your overall submission for media trips focused on deep water and river cruises.

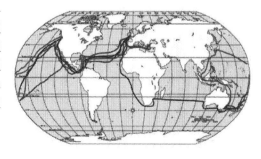

Try to match your travels with photographs. This will help support your travel claims and prove you were there.

Here's a sample listing of numeric detail you should record about your own travels. This information adds to your travel provenance.

1.  You have been in the travel industry for ____ years

2.  You have travelled to ____ countries, places...

3.  You have flown _____ miles, taken _____ cruises...

4.  You have gained your CTA, CTC, MCC, ACC, ECC...

5.  You are a Destination Specialist for _____

6.  You own, manage, work for _____

7.  You specialize in _____

8.  You have sold this many trips _____ during your career

---

Do you sound credible? What else could you list? This is not about boasting; it is about writing down your travel history – where you have been, what you have seen, done and accomplished.

Some of your readers would have travelled way more than you, but don't let that put you off. If they have something to say, why not interview them? Use customer content to fill out your next article.

# YOUR JOURNEY AS A TRAVEL WRITER

What a wonderful idea to be travelling and writing for money, fame and fortune and guess what, it's wide open to you and once you start, you will indeed be thinking what's written below.

Your focus is on writing about your travels in order to increase your sales. However, you might have other ideas.

As you think about your business model and your client list, give some thought to what it is you want your travel writing to do for you.

You might just want to branch out into full-time travel writing or try another idea: plan FIT groups for your clients who like to write and journal about their own trips. Imagine, Literary Tours, booked through you of course. This idea is not new. It's been done before, BUT, how about going with the tech-flow and putting together a tour for Kindle readers. What are they reading on their Kindle as you travel to the first destination? Your e-Book of course!

# WHAT DO YOU WANT YOUR
# TRAVEL WRITING TO DO FOR YOU?

Here are ten possible outcomes. Use them to prompt your own ideas. Read through the list of possibilities and highlight anything that has meaning to your writing career.

| | | |
|---|---|---|
| 1. | **Create a NEW travel niche** | Perhaps you already serve a niche market. Let's say you focus on selling France. During your travels to France you discover a unique village in a particluar region. You have found a niche within a niche to write about. |
| 2. | **Boost revenues on generic trips** | Here you write about the generic sun, sand and sea vacations in such an alluring way that the reader is attracted to book with you and even join your group tour after you wrote about group rates. |
| 3. | **Attract new sales / new customers** | Perhaps your writing focus is writing about YOU and your services and what you can do for the reader. Building credibility and confidence in your existing, new, and referred clients. |
| 4. | **Be paid to travel** | This is a switcheroo. Usually, you will pay the supplier to take you away. In this scenario, your writing is attracting suppliers who invite travel writers on all expense paid FAM/media trips. Your preferred suppliers and departments of tourism already do this. They need to know you are writing. |

| 5. | **Author a book** | This is everyone's dream. In this case it would be a book about your travels. Be cautioned though, as author, Anthony Dalton, often says: "After the first 1,000 words... what then?" |
|----|-------------------|---|
| 6. | **Be paid to speak** | Build your reputation and be ready to quote a fee to speak. Once you become recognized as a travel writer, you will receive offers to speak. A starting fee would be $500-$800 + expenses. Eventually, you will be at $5,000. |
| 7. | **Start a blog** | You may already have an agency blog – if you do not, you might want to start one and use your blog to launch your new career. |
| 8. | **Start a newsletter** | Most agencies offer a newsletter. The question is - do they inspire travel? If you wrote it, could you boost agency sales? |
| 9. | **Start a magazine** | Easy to do. Type in Word. Save as a PDF and upload to the e-magazine website of your choice. Why not start out as a contributor to an existing travel trade magazine? |
| 10. | **Enter and win competitions** | A great way to win travel prizes, money and to gain recognition and fame. Looks good on the writing bio/profile too. |

# CREATE A LOGO FOR YOURSELF

You are going to need a logo to represent your travel writing and thank goodness you do not need to spend thousands of dollars to have your logo designed. You can use the program I use for all my logo creations, and here it is – The Logo Creator 7.

Here's a logo I created for myself. I use this one when I'm promoting my photography that I've turned into an art form.

Your travel writing logo will help readers identify your work. If you are or will be writing under the brand of the agency you work for, you'll need to discuss whether you use the agency logo or your own. This is important. If you take off and just do your own thing, it will not sit well with senior management.

https://www.laughingbirdsoftware.com/

# CLEARANCE TO WRITE

As an employee of a travel agency, what you write would normally be the property of the agency. Make sure you have full and legal clearance to claim yourself as the author of what you write. You'll want to own the copyright to what you write.

If you do write under the banner of your agency, you must write in accordance with the style and requirements set by the agency owner.

If the agency owner agrees that you can write for the agency but use your own name and logo, why not create your own blog or webpage on the agency website? In this way, you will have an instant readership. Remember you are not writing to the agency clientele in order to steal away their bookings sometime down the road. That is illegal and prison food ain't good! You are writing to the agency clientele to help increase overall agency sales and at the same time, boost your writing career and earnings.

Include your photography too and make sure each image carries your name. If photography is more your strength then why not open accounts with Flickr for instance.

Either way, make sure you create a recognizable logo. It's part of your branding. It should set you aside as a travel selling writer. You want readers and clients to recognize your logo, follow your writing career and then book their trips with you.

## WHAT EDITORS WANT

To understand what editors want is to read through dozens of websites, explore every link possible and get to grips with the travel media/publishing industry. Most publications are looking for something new and very, very exciting – not regurgitated material from tourism websites. To meet their demands, you might want to take one or two creative writing courses unless you have a natural talent.

If you plan on being published, then you must adhere to the rules and terms of what your publisher is asking of you and from you. If you do not, then your submission will go in the bin!

Read the NY Times Submission Guidelines below, and you will see that they are not interested if your writing has a promotional slant to it – so let's say a supplier sent you on a FAM, and in your piece, you mention them more than the destination. Your submission in this instance is going in the bin again! They also want new stuff, not repurposed or revamped articles from three years ago.

# The New York Times
**Submission Guidelines**
**Please do not send photos.**

1.  The Travel Section will not publish articles that grow out of trips paid for or in any way subsidized by an airline, hotel, tourist board or other organization with an interest, direct or indirect, in the subject of an article.

2.  We buy all rights to articles and will not purchase a piece that has been published elsewhere...

For full submission guidelines visit this webpage:
http://www.nytimes.com/ref/travel/SUBMISSION.html

## GoNOMAD

Let's take a look at the Writer's Guidelines found on the GoNOMAD.com website. GoNOMAD knows precisely what they want from you, and typical submissions will not win the day. They don't want fluff or extra fluff! Here's a paragraph from the GoNOMAD website. Visit the link for more information.

---

# Become a Travel Writer For GoNOMAD!

GoNOMAD prides itself on providing excellent, entertaining, informative and unique travel articles and research about destinations, activities, and experiences. No glossy magazine fluff, no standard guidebook descriptions, no promotional hype; just honest, accurate, well-written and detailed articles and destination guides that speak to an educated, curious and well-travelled audience.

https://www.gonomad.com/travel-writer-guidelines

That is a great logo! Love it.
Look for logos like this one when you start to create your own.
You will gain inspiration.

## NATIONAL GEOGRAPHIC WRITER'S GUIDELINES

To be published in National Geographic is probably every professional travel writer's dream. When you land on the National Geographic site for writers, here's what will greet you:

# How to Pitch Nat Geo Travel
### Have a great idea? We want to hear it!

## OUR CURRENT PRIORITIES RIGHT NOW (CHECK BACK FOR UPDATES).

- Experts to write fun guide pages with local tips for: Denver, Austin, Santa Barbara, Portland, Dallas, and Phoenix

- Geographic diversity: pitches about the Caribbean, Central America, Middle East and Africa

NG's requirements change. They ask the reader to check back. When you visit this webpage, there's plenty more to read. The link is long, so you can search for NG How to Pitch and that should get you there.

https://www.nationalgeographic.com/travel/features/how-to-pitch-nat-geo-travel-pitching-guidelines/

## HERE'S A GREAT LIST FROM THEWRITELIFE WEBSITE

# 34 Travel Magazines and Websites That Pay Freelance Writers
https://thewritelife.com/travel-freelance-writers/

# YOU: THE EDITOR & THE PUBLISHER

Now you know: if you submit your writing to magazines you do not own, you will be required to conform to their standards, terms and conditions. All of which makes sense from their point of view. They need to control what they accept, print and publish. Job done.

But what about you writing for you? Things change when you strike out on your own and publish your own e-magazine. Technology favours all new independent publishers (referred to as Indie) like yourself. If you wish, you can publish your articles in your very own digital magazine, and you can also submit your work to be published in other media, too. Moreover, the best thing is – you can blend the two.

You may decide to write for 'them' as you learn your craft and then branch out when you feel you are ready to write for 'you'. On the other hand, you may wish to stay with 'them' and avoid the hassles of self-publishing. Writing for 'them' builds recognition and lays the foundation you will need for when you do self-publish.

Once you launch your own publication and grow your readership, you might be in the ballpark to entice travel suppliers to advertise in your magazine, on your blog, your webpage and throughout your social media activity.

Today the choice is yours. Depending upon your travel writing goal, either route will get you somewhere. Our preferred 'somewhere' and still the focus of this book, is to have you profit from new travel sales enhanced by your writing.

The quickest route to profit would be to write for your travel agency clients and their friends and write about what it is you want to sell them.

The following chart presents the pros and cons of you writing for 'them' and you writing for 'you.'

| WRITING FOR THEIR MEDIA | WRITING FOR YOUR MEDIA |
|---|---|
| 1. Quality media brand | 1. Immediately accepted |
| 2. Builds recognition | 2. Your rules |
| 3. Attracts editors to call | 3. Your guidelines |
| 4. Helps editors accept | 4. Your deadlines |
| 5. Many refusals | 5. Builds recognition for YOU |
| 6. Many rules to follow | 6. Attracts editors |
| 7. Guidelines | 7. Attracts advertisers |
| 8. Deadlines | 8. ROI in booking revenues |
| 9. No money to some money | 9. Build the reputation you want |
| 10. Eventually big money! | 10. Open an E-Store – to sell your written works |

## Writing to Increase Bookings

Writing to client base means you can write to suit current market and travel trends and attract your clients, and their travelling friends, to book with you. An article on The Joy of Cruising might boost cruise bookings.

Whatever you write should be worthy of being forwarded (viral) by email and social media. It should read so well, be so inspiring, your clients will want to share it with their friends. Remember the submission mantra: inspire readers to follow in the writer's footsteps.

If you own or manage a $3 to $5 million travel agency and you serve 500 active clients from an overall customer list of 1500, you will, or you should be able to generate new sales from your travel writing as it inspires your clients to travel once again. As you build a reputation, fame and fortune should follow, and that reputation remains one of your travel writing goals.

You will need a good copy editor regardless of how well you write. Having an editor on your team will allow you to travel more, write more and generate more sales from your travel writing. Whatever your editor costs, it will be a sound investment. You cannot do it all as you already know. If you have the editing skills then in the short term you can do it. Later as your time is taken up with travel, writing and selling, you should outsource the editing.

## Issuu.com

Here's where you can publish your first eBook, e-Magazine, e-Anything! The basic accounts are FREE, and the Pro account will cost you a small monthly fee. The ISSUU publishing platform is fantastic. As you can see below, I used it for my Selling Travel magazine. So easy to set up. Visit: www.issuu.com

## Joomag.com

This publishing site is similar to ISSUU however you can insert video on a Joomag page, and the reader can play that video from that page. In other words, the reader does not leave your magazine. But wait, there's more!

The Joomag interface not only allows you to add video, but you can also create a 2-page spread which is terrific for your wide-angle photography. www.joomag.com

Below is one of my Joomag magazines, on the page titled The NEXT Screen, you can see the video box ready to be clicked and watched. That's what YOU can produce and publish. Back up your writing with video. Fantastic!

# WHAT TO LOOK FOR WHEN TRAVELLING

When you are travelling, look for the things, people, places and ideas you can write about that will increase your travel sales. Of course the information you gather will also be used in a generic travel article. However when you write to grow your travel sales, there's more to it.

You should be looking for where the "value for money" resides and think from your client's point of view. You will also want to expose the best side of those preferred suppliers you recommend and sell.

**Travelling for yourself:** Look for different opportunities to write about and focus your content on the all-purpose travel reader – still, however with a dollar figure in mind. The generic travel article is intended to build interest followed by inquiry, followed by a sale. If you write beyond the affordability of your clients, then your articles will miss the mark. You cannot pitch luxury cruises to the client who only wants to spend two-thousand dollars.

Writing as, You Inc., you will no doubt concentrate on your passion, your niche, your dream trip and then share this information with would-be clients. Some may follow you, others will read and stay put.

**Travelling on a FAM:** Your FAM focus will be on in-flight service, hotel service, amenities, getting 'there,' features, benefits, value for money, local deals and local advice and of course, about the supplier.

---

## Are you listed with all suppliers, for all FAMs?

---

Have you planned your FAM PLAN for the current and coming year? Where would you like to travel to, when and with which supplier? You will need this plan so that you can schedule your writing, your topics, when to publish and you must also factor in selling time. As an independent contractor time is you own. As an agency employee with limited time to travel, you should create a FAM PLAN.

# THINK FOR YOUR READER

Time to think about your readership. Who would most likely be your reader? Chances are they would be your existing clients and also those who have opted-in to your email list or newsletter list – PLUS your social network contacts. You must factor in all those who might be following you, connecting to you, liking you, friending you, tweeting about you. Your social connections are the route to your writing being forwarded. Going, going, gone viral is action you need to have happen.

## You have two questions to answer:

| Who is your reader now? | Whom do you want as a reader? |
|---|---|
| • newsletter recipients | • new niche client |
| • your social network | • the travel trade |
| • existing clients | • colleagues / management |
| | • travel magazine readership |

The left column is asking you to think about your current readership, or from where you could attract an immediate readership.

The right-hand column is asking you to project forward to the future and the readership/audience you want to attract by design. Perhaps as you read more about what editors want from you, you will be able to use those same parameters for when you write for yourself.

A recent poll of what travellers are most interested in had nothing to do with sunsets and around the world trips. What 'everyone' wanted to know, believe it or not, related to bathrooms, cleanliness, safety and security. After that, it's down to the beach, or museums, or art galleries or trekking, or your niche. Keep this advice in mind. The core essentials are always essential. Clean toilets!

Naturally, when writing for yourself, you will factor in a sales angle related to pricing, departures and again, that special niche you like to sell.

# WHAT TO WRITE, WHEN AND TO WHOM

Deciding what to write, when and to whom will force you to examine your passion, your list of unusual places, things you know, and even stuff you have wanted to share for some time. Your travel philosophy for instance. What is it? Can you share it? Write about it?

The **WHAT** refers to your knowledge. Do you have in-depth information and research to support your writing? **The WHEN** is all about seasonality, or as soon as you get back from wherever you have been. **The WHOM** has to be your current client list which will expand the more you write and publish and build a readership.

The **WHAT-Part Deux:** What to write? It's a tough question. However, we can try to trim the width a little to something manageable. In the left-hand column below the first listing reads Cruising Safety. A hot topic. Since the Concordia capsize, there have been many more cruise related incidents, and they continue to happen. Review the list below and let your topic ideas flow.

| | |
|---|---|
| Cruising safety | Travel for single women |
| Airline fees | What to pack |
| New destinations | Travel gadgets |
| Eco anything | Family travel |
| Green travel | Weddings & meetings at sea |
| Adventure travel | Travel apps for smartphones |

Do you have a particular travel passion you can write about? A special place you would like to share and then escort a high priced tour there?

- What's YOUR passion?
- Where is YOUR special place?
- That fling, thing. Remember?
- What season is coming up?

**Keep thinking about what's in your travel soul that you can write about and not just one article, but ongoing.**

## Beware the Fluff

I am sure you have read more than your share of travel journals and blogs, and at times the writer is so wrapped up in trying to win the World Prize for Writing Fluff they have lost you in the overworked phrasing.

That is not what you want to do. The best thing for you to do is to develop your style, a style that suits your readership, or the readership you intend to target. Now, some readers may desire fluff. However, it is safe to say that most readers want to experience what you have experienced as expressed through your written word and images.

Write so you pull the reader into your article. Engage the reader using powerful words and phrasing. Read the text below: it tells us about what you saw, were looking at, the scent of the flowers. The reader is with you, stopping their bike with you and imagining that field of wild flowers.

*We saw the field ahead. Stopped cycling to look at the amazing landscape covered in wildflowers – such a glorious scent...*

Here then, if this is your style, less is more. You may choose to use fluffy prose if that is what your readership demands. Work your magic to lead the reader from start to finish without getting them lost along the way. If you do take a diversion make sure it is clear to the reader so they can go with you, follow you.

Writing beautiful prose and descriptive phrases are not what I call fluff. You will know when a travel writer is writing to themselves. My style is usually clipped, fast and to the point. Not everyone's cup of tea. So you must always develop your own style. Change it, reinvent it as needed. Get to the point where your readers are shouting for more.

# THE MARKETPLACE

As a travel writing travel agent the marketplace is wide open to you and for a number of reasons – the main one is this:

## Writing is not easy, and people tend to give up.

A second reason would be: very few travel agents are travel writers in the truest sense of the title. The opportunity is yours if you can hang in there and learn the craft.

If you do hang in there, take your lumps, keep trying, learn to improve, find your angle and stick with it – then you will make something happen for yourself in the literary travel circles, boosting your travel sales in the process – your primary goal.

Choosing your piece of the marketplace pie is essential. I decided to write about what comes naturally to me which is new business generating ideas, how they work in the travel trade and how to implement them. I write to and for the travel trade. That makes me a B2B writer. Your end-reader would more than likely be the consumer – you would be a B2C writer.

The B2B door is also open to you. If you are excellent at what you sell, then write about how you do it and build a travel trade readership.

The only downside, writing to your fellow agent, is that you are not writing to an audience who will purchase travel from you. However, you could generate additional income from your trade colleagues when you write and publish how-to books and manuals that your fellow associates can purchase and apply your knowledge to boost *their* sales.

If your travel trade how-to books do well, you might be invited to speak at travel trade conferences for a fee. Nice! That will get your adrenaline pumped beyond normal and add to your bank balance too.

Let's explore current readership and new opportunities:

| Readership | New Opportunities |
|---|---|
| • Clients | • Tell/sell what you know |
| • Consumers | • Teach how you do it |
| • Trade – general | • Create newsletters |
| • Trade - colleagues | • Write for social networks |
| | • Write a trade blog |

**Readership:** Are you connected to a host group or consortium? If so, you may have a few hundred travel agents who are already related to you and would support your travel writing and how-to publications. It is worth thinking about and chatting with head office on how you can earn money writing to and for the membership.

**New Opportunities:** The New Opportunity list is waiting for you if you can stand on stage in front of a large audience and entertainingly deliver your ideas. If you do this, remember your audience will also include younger, tech-savvy travel agents. There is no way you can pretend you know how to use Facebook or Instagram for instance. Do that, and the audience will keep you honest.

The Baby Boomer travel agent is still out there, alive and well and selling. Never forget this trailblazing segment of the trade and what their current knowledge needs are.

If you are going to write about social media and trending apps, then make sure you have created accounts, tested all the features and understand the benefits. You should also be able to demonstrate how each app works in real time. Remember the key point here is to show you know. Focus on the HOW not the WHAT.

# BEFORE YOU LEAVE

When travelling by yourself, for yourself, one of the most important things to take with you is an idea of what you intend to write about, a story idea, a focus.

If you are contracted to write on behalf of a supplier or trade magazine, then your topic will be presented to you before you go or at least you will have a remit to accomplish.

Having your topic set before you leave allows you to focus and not be distracted by all those sights and sounds that might lead you astray. Chances are however you will fit them all in and bring home enough content for more than one article. The extra information is useful for your submission bank – the folder that contains ready-to-send articles should writer's block ever set in.

Carry a planned itinerary, a list of contacts, a list of questions and if you have made any appointments, record the time and date, place, contact phone numbers and email addresses.

Be sure to have a backup plan should your laptop die. Paper still works! Don't forget apps such as Dropbox. You will need a central place to go should your tech fail. You can access your Dropbox files from your tablet, phone or internet cafe.

## What's In Your Tote Bag?

The tools of your new trade should include:

1. Laptop / tablet
2. Smartphone + Dragon Naturally Speaking voice-to-text app
3. Apps – GPS, Maps
4. Voice recording app
5. Pen/pencil, notepad

Always a good idea when travelling by yourself is to pre-hire a tour guide so you can get to places you might not have access to on your own. If language is a barrier, your tour guide will assist.

Suggest you work with the tourism office to find your tour guide. They may offer someone from their own roster – free of charge if you are lucky. Also, tour guides recommended by the tourism office, are certified so you should not have any challenges. As a female, if you are nervous about travelling to unfamiliar territory with a male guide, request a female tour guide. Safety first is always the number one box to be ticked.

Wearing a t-shirt like the one shown here makes for a conversation starter with locals and tourists.

# ASKING QUESTIONS - GETTING FACTS

To get the local scene down on paper or typed into your device means interviewing people and asking questions. Your list of pre-arranged questions will be helpful. You should have your central questions memorized so you can handle what would appear to be an impromptu interview.

When interviewing on the street, you can equip yourself with a t-shirt and business cards. Have a prepared introduction to what you are doing and writing about so when you engage with a tourist, and chat with locals, you can quickly put them at ease.

Be prepared for a formal sit down chat with the hotel general manager and local tourism officials. This would be a different situation compared to the casual interaction with tourists. It would be friendly but more formal. Before you meet with anyone in an official capacity, you would be expected to have done your homework. Check the dress code too.

The hard facts can be found on the supplier's website. When you are on location you will be researching in real time: why people go there, come here, what they like about the place, the venue, their top three places to eat and so on.

Depending on your special interest, you might also be searching around for the best place to shop, the level of danger in climbing to the top of the local mountain, if adventure is your niche. If food is on your menu – where to find the best local snacks.

One way to learn the craft of on-location interviewing is to watch television interviewers at work. You can try out their techniques as you walk the local coffee shops, bars and pubs for local input.

There are plenty of travel shows on television that you can learn from. Listen to the host as they question local travel guides and talk about the history, the food, where to go and so on. You can start with Rick

Steves. He is always asking questions based on his TV audience. Likewise, you would ask questions your readers would ask.

## Tell Me...

The latest questioning technique that has become TV interviewer's favourite is: "Tell me..." and it's not even a question, it's a request, here it is again: "Tell me..." and when interviewing on behalf of your video fans, you would change it to: "Tell us..."

Now you add the ending to that "Tell me..." introduction, such as:

- Tell me when...

- Tell me about...

- Tell us how you felt when you first...

- Tell me how it all happened when...

- Tell us more about...

Right, off you go. Start listing your "Tell me..." questions. Be sure to change the intro from time to time otherwise you will sound like a looped recording.

Remember to check into what you should *not* to talk about. Usually politics and religion. You must be sensitive to these issues; however if you are writing about religious tours for instance, then you should be cleared to ask your questions as long as they do not challenge local beliefs.

# HOW IMAGERY FACTORS INTO YOUR SALES

To help boost your readership and travel sales you might want to support your travel writing with your own photographic images, video or both.

When you shot the image or you arrange for someone else to take the photo with you in the picture, it adds credibility to your article. The concept of being there, on-site, as you wrote about your experience has a better chance of being credible when you are actually in the picture. You do not need to be in every shot. Just one or two would suffice. No need for the lolling tongue or devil's horns hand signs! Unless that is relished by your readership.

It is a mistake to say or believe you are not photogenic, or you do not like your photo taken. It is a must do. No complaints. Learn the craft of setting up the shot and get right into the centre of the image. Learn which side is your best side. Study your facial expressions, shoot hundreds of images until you know how you look from different angles and how to dress for all sorts of occasions. Learn which colour suits your complexion.

Don't forget the shots where you can have some fun and spoof yourself in certain situations. Readers enjoy good clean humour and a joke here and there.

Keep in mind what we are working towards: you as a travel agent, writing about your travels to generate more travel sales and hopefully spin-off a new career at the same time. You will want to be professional in all aspects, even when spoofing. Excellent photography will boost your chances of being read.

## Imagery Ideas

| | |
|---|---|
| Photographs | Sketches |
| Posters | Watercolours |
| Video | Combinations |
| FX'd images | Artwork |

The image shown above is one of mine. A sketch that I photographed then turned into a poster using the Adobe Photoshop Elements software. The cost of PSE is around $100. Very affordable.

Perhaps you are artistic and like to draw – well why not support your article with a sketch – and, if it works for you, photograph your drawing and posterize it or use the watercolour filter. Anything to be different but an image that still represents where you were and what you are writing about. You might be a pen and ink artist. If so that is fantastic. Include your sketch. Once again your readership will appreciate the fact that you were there and took the time to produce an original artwork. Whichever route you choose, the whole idea of supporting your writing with imagery is one more key to your success.

Now, as you may or may not know, many people are more interested in viewing a short video than reading a blog. They want that multimedia experience. Today, video production is as easy as holding up your smartphone and pressing the record button. The video quality is good enough for your intended use which is to add video to support your blog or webpage where your articles are read. If you publish a magazine on Joomag, then you would insert your travel video into your Joomag page.

# YOUR OWN YOUTUBE CHANNEL

Video is KING. Yes, it is. It is the best format for promoting travel and if the number of videos played each day on Facebook and YouTube is anything to go by, well, that is one bandwagon you should be jumping on. You may prefer another video outlet/app and that is okay. Just remember, the masses view Facebook and YouTube.

Using video as your number one writing, blogging, vlogging tool is easy to do – but tough to do well. On the other hand, you are not trying to become a Hollywood producer. However, you could be looking at becoming a Photo Journalist.

Whether or not video is your number one form of imagery to support your writing, open an account with YouTube and create your own travel channel.

Once your channel is in place, you can upload your edited videos from wherever you are in the world and then email or post to your social media accounts. Post a note to your readership to visit your YouTube channel and to watch your latest video. If you blog, then your video can be embedded into your blog. A link can also be embedded into your online article or typed out in the printed version. In PDF format, links are live and clickable.

Use video to promote your next article, or the destination itself. Set up promotional event for when you return to the office by advising your viewership to "wait two more days…" when you will be back in the office, arranging a presentation. In the meantime, offer a link to where your audience can click to view more, read more and check out your photographs. Link your social media activity to your digital media to your printed media. Tie it all together. Give your readership the options they want.

Check out each of the eleven channels listed at the link below. See what you like, dislike and learn from each channel.

11 Inspiring YouTube Travel Channels to Follow

https://theplanetd.com/youtube-travel-channel/

To open your YouTube channel, you must have a Google account. Visit www.youtube.com and create your channel by typing in your Google information and you are on your way!

**Get Smart:** Check your smartphone. Does it have the best-of-best camera and camera apps? If not, time to upgrade.

Let your smartphone capture your images and video – especially videos of you chatting with locals and travel trade contacts. Make sure you carry a light but sturdy tripod. Shaky videos will not bode well for your writing vlogging career.

Check the camera settings and shoot quality footage in 1080 HD, 4K or better. The lower settings will not deliver the right video quality for your use. As and when you convert to various formats, you will want the original video to be best-of-best. FYI: Panasonic Lumix cameras that shoot 4K, have an option to stop at any frame and capture it as an image.

# SHOOTING THE STORY

It is quite possible that you may prefer not to write but to video everything. You will capture sights and sounds for future reference and once edited you will have your latest journey ready to upload to your VLOG (video blog). If the video is crisp and clear, then you can also isolate the screen and save still shots from the same video. Most current video production and editing software programs offer this feature. You can research Pinnacle Studio by Corel.

A video blog: where you once wrote, you now video. Where your readers once read, they now watch. This is the way to go, and most travel suppliers and tourist offices already have their video platforms established online. For the best of all worlds, why not combine the two – text blog and video.

To shoot the story, you will need additional tools. They are not expensive if you start using your smartphone as your video camera. Here's where you start:  http://photojojo.com/store/

At the Photojojo online store, you will find what you need to stabilize your smartphone and that means purchasing a bracket or clamp for your tripod. Visit www.joby.com/store for the tripod.

You will need a boom microphone that plugs into your phone or tablet.

A set of lenses to attach to your phone's camera helps you zoom and shoot wide angle. If you upgrade your phone, then chances are your new phone has everything you need such as twin lenses for zooming and portraiture. For a sneaky shot of someone in the marketplace, there is a right-angled mirror lens for your DSLR.  Referred to as a spy lens.

Using your smartphone as a photographic tool is known as phoneography, and you can search online for more information on how best to use your phone as your main investigative camera.

You might be interested in the iPhoneography course found at this link: http://photojojo.com/university/

## iPhoneography links to explore

The iPhone has its own set of supporters and websites that can deliver everything you need to know about using your iPhone as your main camera when travelling and shooting to support your article.

http://www.iphoneographycentral.com/
https://iphonephotographyschool.com/iphoneography-websites/

---

## Below is my kit for when I am on assignment.

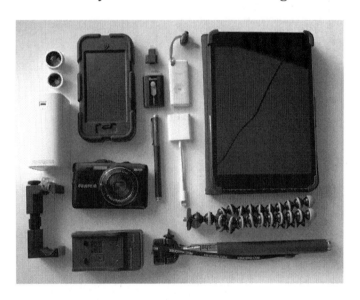

Lenses, power booster, clamps, iPhone, pocket camera, charger, mini drive, pen, remote, iPad, tripod, selfie stick.

# VIDEO SITE FINE PRINT

You should be aware of the Terms and Conditions, i.e. the *fine print* when uploading your videos to sites like YouTube and Vimeo. Some conditions allow, in this case, Vimeo, to use your video content. You retain ownership. However, Vimeo is permitted to use your video as they explain at the link below.

https://vimeo.com/terms

YouTube has similar terms and conditions. If you do not want your video used in this way, then you must upload your videos to your own channel and check the PRIVATE box. If the public box is checked, then everyone can view it. You can be selective as to which video you want to be seen by a worldwide audience.

https://www.youtube.com/static?gl=CA&template=terms

Whichever video outlet you use, be sure to read their Terms and Conditions online and make sure their rules and regulations will work for you. Read terms related to License to Other Users, Duration of Licenses and Non-video Content.

# CHOOSING YOUR CAMERA

There is no right or wrong choice here. The factors that will help you decide the type and style of camera you choose will be determined by the kind of articles you intend to write, the type of images you plan to shoot and how much baggage and equipment you want to carry.

Your generic smartphone can do it all for you, and if you download specific photo apps, then you can even edit on the go. Here's my iPhone7 Plus with hard screen protector and hard rubber casing with lanyard loop – and that lanyard is very, very important. It will prevent you from dropping your phone into that deep, deep chasm. Also, with the phone tethered to your wrist, it cannot be stolen.

Your smartphone can produce both quality images and 'snapshot photography' which would serve more as a record of your trip versus supporting your article in print or online.

If your idea is to shoot and sell more images then writing articles then naturally you will be looking for the best DLSR you can afford. Most of the top rated DLSRs now shoot 1080 and or 4K video as do most of the smaller digital cameras. Professional grade imagery will require a quality semi-pro camera such as Canon, Nikon, Sony and Lumix. The choice of extra lenses is yours. Wide angle to zoom.

When I am flying overseas, I tend to go with my iPhone and a small but powerful point and shoot like a Lumix. I save the heavy duty cameras for road trips. The weight of the camera plus all the lenses and the additional kit is just one of those things to factor in when you are on an assignment. If one camera can do it all and do it well, then that is probably the one you take with you.

The semi-pro camera will be an excellent investment should you be thinking of selling your images online from your website or through a stock photo agency website.

There are dozens of apps for you to choose from should you wish to edit as you go and upload directly to your social networks. Most existing built-in apps are all you need to produce a reasonable image and record of your travels.

## FOCOS App

Just found this app. It is for phones with twin lenses and works especially well for portraits. You can even alter the point of focus after the shot – great for blurring landscape foreground.

## The Sony QX100 / QX10 Lens for Smartphones

This lens came on the scene in 2013. If you can find one, they attach to your smartphone and synch with your camera apps. You can hold the lens in your hand to shoot around corners, over the heads of the crowd and all the time view what the camera "sees" on your phone.

Let's move on to the latest and greatest form of photography and videography: drones.

## Drones and Your Next Article

Perhaps you have a passion for photography, and you would like to write about it. Travel photography will never go out of print. So there is a career for you. The latest development in camera tech is, of course, the drone. A travel writer with a drone is something to consider. Have drone will travel – the wonder of technology. You can go pro, or you can go selfie.

You will be aware of all the types of drones that are flying the skies, and you will be thinking they are large, professional and you will need a few thousand dollars in your jeans to buy one. That is true for the pro versions. But wait, check these out:

## Zerotech Dobby Mini Selfie Pocket Drone

This one is the size of your phone. Fits in your jean pocket. It is the Zerotech Dobby Mini Selfie Pocket Drone with 13MP High Definition Camera U.S. Version with Official Warranty. Price $195

### Parrot Disco FPV

What if you could buy a small professional drone for under $700? Here's one I found that is stylin'. You simply toss it in the air and off it goes. The Parrot Disco FPV – Easy to fly fixed wing drone, up to 45 minutes of flight time, 50 mph top speed, FPV goggles. Price $699

# USING YOUR TRAVEL WRITING & PHOTOGRAPHS TO SELL MORE TRAVEL

There are so many outlets through which you can share your story and get the message out that you have travelled, returned and have something to say and images to show. The challenge is getting a foot in their door. So we focus on YOU developing your own media outlets.

Keep the focus on yourself and your travels and what you want to promote and then sell to your clients. When you are actively writing and posting your travel articles, your clients will be pre-sold in many cases and just wait for your tell-all presentation. It is at that presentation, where you close the sale. Online, you can present using Facebook to run a live show or host the event in your agency, at a local hotel or library.

Wherever you host the presentation always factor in a Buy Now campaign. Your preferred suppliers will most surely join you in this promotion and especially if you are going to sell some seats.

Email is perhaps the easiest and fastest way to get your articles published and out to your readership. You can do this before or as soon as you return. You could offer a link to past articles, current video footage and your most recent presentation if you recorded it. Attach your article in various formats such as PDF.

## PDF to Kindle
Many of your readers will be using a Kindle eReader so you should be ready to explain how your clients can download your article to their Kindle. Here's one link that describes how:

https://www.wikihow.com/Add-a-PDF-to-a-Kindle

## Word2Kindle.com

This is an excellent service. Nick Caya is the owner, and he will receive your Word document and convert it to ePUB and MOBI which means you can publish on Kindle. Basic conversion cost is $49. Fees go up based on the number of images and fancy layouts.

## 16 forms of communication:

1. e-mail
2. newsletters
3. websites
4. blogs
5. eBooks
6. press releases
7. webinars
8. texting
9. social media
10. e-magazines
11. video
12. apps
13. podcasts
14. Skype
15. TV
16. messaging

As each new article becomes more exciting and believable, your customers will want to read YOU, and they will be waiting for your next issue. As you can see above, you have a choice of channels through which to communicate your message. When you send your post trip article by e-mail, you intend to entice them to make contact. Be sure to ask them to do just that.

If you use an email service such as Mail Chimp or Constant Contact, choose a template that offers you a layout featuring an image placement. The insert the image that best supports your article. That image might be just enough to boost the readership and nudge those readers to inquire and book with you.

Also listed in your post trip e-mail will be a link to where your previous articles can be found. Invite your readers to a presentation. Mention your new book and create a signature title for yourself such as: "Travel Writer." Don't get too fancy. Keep it real.

Although the travel chatter is about using social media, e-mail is still the number one tool in the digital tool box which means you will want to continue using it and blend its use into your social media activities.

We also know that 99% of people online use email which means you can pretty much send your travel writing updates to anyone with access to the internet via their favourite gadget.

If your new article is compelling and supported by excellent photography or video, then chances are you will generate new bookings for your tours. What if your article encouraged at least five to ten readers to book their travel with you or to register for your next tour? Not a bad return if that happens.

---

*A KEYPOINT – at this moment in time you are building a readership from your known customer list. Later on, we will discuss how you can build a readership external to your agency list.*

---

Quite simply, if you do write a compelling, been-there-done-that, been-there-survived-this, article, AND you had an angle, a story, a new twist on cruising and you wrote it in a humourous style – then you will attract people to read more of YOUR work. A little humour goes a long way.

And once that audience becomes fans, those fans will eventually book their travel with you. Your target audience for these articles would be your current clients. To use the current social media term you have created your very own *engagement* program.

You have established your audience and although you think you know them – you may have to profile them a little more.  Listen to how they speak, the words and phrasing they use. Sometimes you must write to your audience in the language they use and understand and then later; you can woo them over to your style of writing.

You also have the option of just going for it, and come out swinging with your style and be done with it. However, back to basics: knowing your audience and appealing to their style, needs and wants is usually the place to start.

If you are an agency owner or manager why not write articles featuring members of the agency team. They can be profiled by where they have travelled, the photographs they have taken and by writing and posting this type of article as the owner/manager you can build sales for your agency, too.

You may want to create a Team Article and have each member of your agency write a paragraph or two about their recent trip and encourage clients to make contact.

Perhaps a team newsletter will work for you. Post it to your agency Facebook page and Boost your Post with a $50 spend to increase readership.

## Building a Readership External of Your Agency List
Here's where you should strive to step out of your comfort zone and pitch your travel skills and talents by getting in front of the general public in your local community.

You can do this by speaking at local events, offering to write a column for the local paper, taking a booth at local business events and even inviting yourself to local common-interest groups. For instance, if there is a local gardening club or local photography club, then you can talk about garden tours of Europe or Japan for example. Sharing your photography with the photography club is another way to excite people to follow your written word.

Offer everyone the chance to join you as a client, to subscribe to your newsletters, to buy your latest travel book and generally preach the fact that you are the BEST travel agent in town.

When someone new joins you as a client, ask them for referrals once they have tasted your level of service. Ask them to forward your emails and articles to their friends.

# BLOGGING FOR DOLLARS

If you already write a blog, then you will know the challenges of maintaining it and keeping the content fresh and exciting. If this is your first blog, then you have a couple of decisions to make ranging from how often you will post to your blog, your level of commitment, and the type of content you will use to attract more readers.

## Time Investment

- Daily: Be prepared to invest 2-hours each day, minimum.

- Weekly: A good choice if you are still selling across the desk.

- As and when: Post to your blog ONLY when you have something of interest to report.

- Your commitment level: Most blogs die within a few months if the commitment is low.

- Keeping it fresh: Plan on-going research for excellent content.

- Your ideas for engaging the reader: Weave in video and podcasts.

---

There are thousands of travel blogging sites, and travel blog directories for you to visit and explore. You will quickly find out, as you explore these lists that many blogs re defunct, gone, off the screen and no longer being monitored. The most significant challenge to writing a travel blog is maintaining it, keeping it fresh and exciting and still do your day job – selling travel.

It may suit you better to submit your articles to an existing travel blog. That way you are not having to maintain the blog site or investing quality selling time to promote your blog. If this sounds like a good thing to do then your next move is to locate blogs you can write for.

Look for directories like the one on the Travel and Tourism Guide website. They list 116 travel blogs, and you could add yours to the list. Be sure to review as many of the blogs as you can. Make a note of the layout, theme, and writing/blogging style. Not all links will be active. A reminder about the need for total commitment: having enough active and fresh content to keep your blog going and going. Yes, like the bunny! Here's the Travel and Tourism Guide link.

http://travelandtourismguide.com/travel-blog-directory/

## TravelPod

Here's a site you might be looking for. Only you will know if it has what you need and want. Give it a click and check it out. www.travelpod.com

## TravelBlog

Similar to TravelPod, www.TravelBlog.org offers you a place to create your new blog and typically these websites offer training, workshops, and articles on how you can be a better travel blogger.

## Starting Your Own Blog

Last but not least, why not start your own blog from scratch, using a blogging program such as Blogger. Google owns it, so your Google account gets you in the door. Once you enter your Google information, you will be zapped over to the blogger set up page. Click on settings, follow all the clicks and within the hour, you should have your blog up and running. Visit: www.blogger.com

## Check Your Website

Have you checked to see if your website host offers a blogging page? They might. I use Weebly for my Selling Travel website, and they provide a blogging page. You can post your articles, upload images and insert a video. You can also tag it and keyword it and add RSS.

## Blogging Books

At the risk of repeating the comment, it is easy to start a blog but very difficult to keep it going on a full time basis AND continue to sell travel. However, if you start off on the right foot and follow in the footsteps of successful travel bloggers chances are that blogging and vlogging could turn out to be your best form of promotion to sell more travel.

There are so many books on how to blog that I'd best let you explore online and find the ones that appeal to you. If in doubt, you can always head for the Dummies section. That's right, you can always bank on the For Dummies series to produce a book on the topic, and here it is. As always the Dummies books are thorough. All you will need to do is factor in the topic of travel.

## This just in!

Just read someone's blog, and they happened to replace the 'b' with their own initial. In this case, BLOG became CLOG. It was easy to understand that CLOG meant blog. So, for me, my blog tab should now read SLOG. I kinda like it. It's different. Catchy. Worth a try to check reader's reactions. Some initials may not work: QLOG, XLOG…hmm, you can always go back to BLOG.

# WRITING AND SELLING EBOOKS

With your blogging career underway plus the fact you are still selling travel, your reputation should be growing. Let's assume you are using the tools, books and blogging sites mentioned and contributing to TravelPod.com which is owned by parent company, TripAdvisor. Not a bad combination of companies to be associated with.

Blogging means a potential source of new travel clients and new readers. They will join your blog once you attract them through all the other communication channels your agency uses. First and foremost would be to mention your travel blog on your website and in all emails. If you have a TravelPod account, point your clients to that blog page.

Your blog can now be used to promote your latest travel book or travel guide that you have published as an eBook.

## The eBook

This publishing format has come a long way, and as you know, there are now dozens of eBook readers like Kindle and Kobo plus eBook apps that allow you to read an eBook on your mobile phone, tablet and other handheld devices. Once you write your eBook, there is a significant audience at the other end of those eBook readers and travel blogging websites who might purchase a copy, and better still, book their travel with you.

The most common eBook format is PDF. Write your book in Word (or your word processing program of choice) and then Save/Print to PDF. Now you can upload your new eBook to almost any eBook website, reader or device.

To do this well, purchase a PDF program. Adobe Acrobat is expensive, but hey, you will be making money! A cheaper program and the one I use is: PDF Converter found here: www.nuance.com

Although PDF is the main format for almost every eBook reader the actual format for let's say a Kindle is called ePub and Mobi. You will have to find someone to convert your Word document into one or both of these file formats. I use www.word2kindle.com.

Once you produce your eBook or a series of eBooks, you will look for a place to post them such as this site called, wait for it, www.ebooks.com.

Search for travel books. Purchase one to check out what other travel writers are producing and how the eBooks.com download works. As an author, you will want to click to this link and start reading.

https://www.ebooks.com/information/authors.asp

Don't forget you are self-publishing, so you are the publisher. Some websites ask to do business only with the publisher, not the author. You will have to advise them that you are both.

## Writing for Amazon Kindle

How would you like to generate 70% of the revenue that your eBooks generate when sold via Amazon and read on Kindle?

The answer is: "When do I start?" Visit the link below to read more about how can join the current list of writers, journalists and bloggers who now publish and sell their work on Kindle at Amazon.

https://kdp.amazon.com/self-publishing/help

# THE EBOOK COVER

Chances are you have seen fantastic looking eBook covers. They look like the real thing. Just like a hard or soft cover book. So much so you might look for it at the local book store. The cover design is a crucial component of eBook sales and it is here, creating the cover, that your photography can be used.

You have heard the expression, "You can't tell a book by its cover" well, with that in mind, you will want your eBook cover to resemble the content of what your eBook.

This should not be too difficult if you are, let's say producing an eBook about cruising or hiking in the UK. The title will tell the story. The cover image will support the title. Don't get too fancy with the title and imagery. It might cause the reader to overlook your eBook. Sometimes just text does the job.

Most people go for the "look" of the book first: the colour and layout. Then they read the title and the tag line. If the combination of graphics and book title match what the reader likes, then they will go to the next step, and read further. Eventually, you hope, to click, purchase and download.

I use two programs to create my eBook covers: eCover Software Pro – here's the link: http://ecoversoftwarepro.com/. The other program is called, Box Shot 3D. The cover for my new book, Marketing Ideas (above) was created using Box Shot. https://boxshot.com/

http://ecoversoftwarepro.com/

A typical eBook cover is shown at the angle as you see above. It has a transparent background and sometimes a short shadow and reflection. Most people who shop online know that to read your eBook it must be downloaded, printed or opened onscreen. They know that your cover image is not representing a hard or softcover physical book. However, the look of your cover will still nudge them towards making a purchase.

If you are not artistic, search locally for eBook cover designers and have them create the cover for you. They would also produce the angled 'look' and deliver the cover image in JPEG and PNG formats.

Kindle offers an eBook cover service.

# PRESS RELEASES – A WRITER'S SECRET WEAPON

You have done well. You have travelled. You have created your blog. You have written travel articles and published your eBook. You have taken amazing photographs. Now you must tell the world about yourself and where the consumer can purchase your eBooks.

The Press Release is one of my favourite topics in my sales and marketing workshops. So few travel agents seem to understand how to use this tool. As a travel blogger, eBook publisher, image creator and seller of travel, the press release should be one of your primary marketing tools.

There was a time (and it is still with us) when your press release was subject to the newspaper or magazine editor's decision as to whether or not it would be published. Today, just like self-publishing, you can publish your press releases, anytime. There is no one to stop you from delivering your press or media release. You can send it out using one of the many services that will review and edit your press release for a small fee. These same press release services are connected to mainstream media and social networks. Select the plan that works for you in terms of reach and price. You should still try the "old way" of sending your press release to local and national newspapers and magazines. You never know. They might like it and publish it.

## Press Release Services

Here are two excellent press release services that I have used. Each one has it's own merits and pricing. Be sure to explore both of them. Review their How To Write a Press Release articles and let their editors help you when you need advice.

## The PR Web

Basic package starts at $99 per press release. They have editors to review your release and help you get it right. www.prweb.com

## The PR Log

The basic account is FREE and comes with some advertising. You can also embed a video into your release, and that's FREE too! www.prlog.com

All social media channels are an outlet for your press release. You can post your release, you can link to it and if you wish, record your release on camera and publish a video-release. Check out your favourite social media channels for how they can deliver your press release.

## TravPR

The following is from the TravPR website: "TravPR.com is pleased to offer a premium online press release distribution service for travel and leisure related businesses at a fraction of the price of the larger online PR  services." TravPR is terrific value. For USD$34.95 you can have your press release zapped around the travel universe and then some. www.travpr.com. Keep in mind, your press release is going out to the travel trade and travel media. This might be where you pitch your travel writing services and how-to advice.

---

Do not hesitate to publish a press release. Yes, it must read right, be spell checked, edited and reviewed before being released. Once that is done, you click, you send, and you carry on selling travel. Your press release will surface, and it will advise the recipient how they can find you, read you, follow you and best of all BUY TRAVEL FROM YOU!

# SELF-PUBLISHING WITH ISSUU & JOOMAG

Here is a beautiful self-publishing opportunity that combines your travel writing and your photography. Imagine publishing your digital travel magazine, crammed with your writing. Today, it is as easy as writing your document, then uploading it to your account with Issuu.com or Joomag.com.

Your articles should be saved in PDF format, ready for uploading. Click the upload button and wait a few minutes and there before your very eyes will be your flip page digital e-magazine. How nice is that? You are now a digital magazine publisher. Okay, there are few steps between upload and publish, but truly, it is easy to do.

Once the magazine had been uploaded, to either Issuu or Joomag, you can retrieve a code to embed the magazine into your website. You will also find a Share button where additional links can be copied and applied for direct posts to Facebook and more. The overall opportunities are endless.

Here's my Selling Travel page on Issuu. This is just how your magazine account page would look.

Here's what your published e-magazine would look like full screen. The reader clicks the page to turn it, just like reading travel trade magazines online. The Joomag site and layout is very similar.

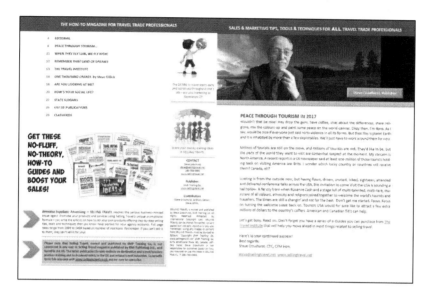

## Selling Your Magazine

Both Issuu and Joomag offer an e-commerce opportunity. That means you price your magazine for sale. When readers want a physical copy, they can purchase it in soft cover. It is not cheap. The reader would pay about $25 for the magazine including postage. Still, it is something to think about as a new source of revenue.

## Video Pages in Joomag

A reminder – the Joomag platform is slightly different to Issuu in that you can embed videos and audio and flash into the digital page. Imagine your reader turning the e-page to find a video of you strolling along a quiet river embankment in France. All they do now is click on the play icon, and your video plays for them within the magazine. Magic! Your reader does not have to sift and sort online – your video is right there. Yes, you can talk to your readers right off the page. Your Joomag issue can also be printed. Joomag uses the same people who print for Issuu. Same costs too.

There is another benefit to publishing your own e-magazine, and that is, once you build the readership to several thousand readers you can approach your preferred suppliers and ask them to advertise with you.

## Writing and Selling Travel Fiction

Stay with me now. We are still focused on generating more travel commissions as the main by-product of your new dual career – travel writing. We have taken a look at blogging, and publishing press releases and publishing your own eBook and e-Magazines. Now, if you truly have a book in you, how about using your travel background as a theme for a novel. *Travel fiction* as the website below states.

Remember those nights in....? And that wonderful moonlit stroll when you... and.... you know... when you shared your life history... and then one thing led to another... and... HOLD IT! Too much information. You can take it from there. Check this opportunity out – see the link below.

http://www.travel-writers-exchange.com

Imagine if this came true. Now you are a travel fiction, or a travel romance writer and how good does that sound? Selling travel, writing novels and building a reader base from your blogs, to your eBooks to your paperbacks and now you are selling upscale and moving those luxury bookings out the door! WOW!

---

Just to show that it can be done, here's my first novel written against the backdrop of 17th century Japan. So, as the saying goes: if I can do it, you can do it, too.

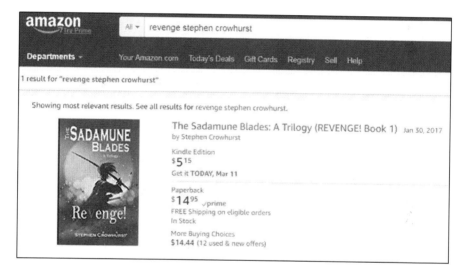

Explore all the 'how to' books and websites you can. Then start writing. Get the story out of your head and down on paper, i.e. on your computer screen. I wrote Revenge on my iPad mini. My passion has always been a combination of Japan and martial arts. Finally, after more than enough years, I got 'er done. It takes time, but it's worth the effort.

Now, back to YOU selling more travel. Once your novel is written, or your guide book for that matter, you can start to make good use of your author status to promote your agency and attract more clients.

# YOUR PHOTOGRAPHIC WINDOW DISPLAY

If you own an agency with a street facing window, try this out. If not negotiate with your agency owner, manager or head office to use the agency window to promote your travel photography. The imagery serves as a call to action. You'll be targeting those consumers driving and walking by your store window. No window? Then you'll be applying this idea to the agency website.

Imagine this is your agency window. That is your photograph framed and hung in the window. It looks wonderful. Consumers are thinking, "I want to go there..." they walk into the agency and start asking questions. I know this works because I have used the idea in my agency.

If your photography is used in this way, the entire agency team can benefit. If you want to focus sell this destination and it is one of your tours that you want to sell, then all the inquiries would come to you.

As you engage the consumer across your desk, you hand them a copy of your latest travel fiction, your business card, (which contains a link to your blog) you mention your website and point out where your articles can be found online. You now have another reader, and hopefully, they will tell their friends. That builds referrals for you. Now, everything you have accomplished regarding writing, taking photographs and blogging, start to converge.

# ENTER TRAVEL WRITING COMPETITIONS

One way to build recognition and to attract people to your travel writing is to enter and win travel writing competitions. Imagine once again, adding a string of wins to your name. What an excellent source of credibility that would be for your travel writing career AND your travel sales.

Travel writing competitions are offered by your preferred suppliers, travel magazines, travel trade magazines and tourism offices too.

There are well-known, annual events that focus on photography. The topic ranges from wildlife to landscape, seascape to you-name-it. Step out of your comfort zone and try it. Test your metal. If you win, you can use that credential forever in your travel writing, business bio and signature.

Even the big guys offer travel writing competitions. National Geographic, many daily newspapers, too. They also offer travel photography competitions. They seem to close out early in the year. Do your due diligence and make sure you have the time to compete.

Send out a press release when you win. Mention you won in your e-magazine, post it on your Facebook business page – tell the world! Travel Agent Wins a Prize for Travel Writing.

# CREATING BUZZ THROUGH SOCIAL MEDIA

It is not required that you become a social media guru, however, it is in your favour to gain a basic understanding of how social media can help improve your readership and your sales.

A couple of things happen when you put your life on the social line. You will most certainly attract readers and new clients, and you will also invite those who like to leave nasty comments. Whether you upload a video or an article, wherever there is a place to leave a comment – someone will. If you are the type of person who takes such things personally, you may be better off restricting the viewing and comments to your clients only. Click on the Private box and remove those nasty people.

Using social media today comes under that old slogan: "You have got to be in it, to win it!" Followed by: "Are you tuff-enough?" If you are good to go, open your social media accounts with Facebook, LinkedIn, Twitter and YouTube or Vimeo and make sure you set up a business page/account versus personal. With Facebook, you will be requested to open a personal page first. After that, you can open a business page. Don't rule out Pinterest, Snapchat and other social media if they make sense and support your goals. You want a return on your account, not "friends" who are not friends.

## Posting to Facebook

Here's where you would type in something about your latest article, and add an image of your publication. You can also include a photo of yourself, writing to entice the reader or a link to your blog or a video. Using a social page like Facebook might just cause your news to go viral as Facebook fans and friends share your information.

Here's a shot of my own "author" Facebook page. The arrow points to the slot where you post your comments.

"Write something" you are prompted. That's a great idea, but what do you write about? Social media gurus tell us, you could be explaining where you are in your new novel. Alternatively, the destination you are visiting. It all takes time, but it's worth the effort. Your intention behind using social media is to prompt your social connections to share your content with their friends. Think viral. What would make your post go viral?

Repeat the above for Twitter. Once you have sent out a Tweet to the Twitterverse you will want that tweet, re-tweeted. Upload that video of you telling your travel story to YouTube and or Vimeo. Once again, direct your listener and reader to where they can read your latest article or blog post. Use #travelwriter or similar.

## The Social Media Dashboard

With so many social activities and messages to track you will need help. If you intend to engage all social media, then it may prove beneficial to open an account with a service such as Hootsuite. Using a service like Hootsuite allows you to manage all of your social media activities from one source. http://hootsuite.com/

# SELLING YOUR NICHE ARTICLES

Next up: niche travel. So what is your niche? Weddings, honeymoons, scuba diving… whatever it is, the fact it is a niche opens more doors for your travel writing and photography. Research which companies and suppliers offer product related to your niche.

Your weddings and honeymoons article might just suit one of the many W&H magazines published each month. Perhaps one of those magazines is looking for travel articles. You never know until you knock on their door. Submit your article and follow up.

Let's go with the weddings and honeymoon niche, and for the niche destination let's make it Italy. Chances are the Italian tourism board has everything they need to promote their own country. Then again, depending on where you travelled to, what you accomplished there and how you wrote about your experiences, perhaps you have found or discovered a new angle to attract honeymooners. If this is the case, then you may have a sale. If you have supporting imagery and video, so much the better.

Based on those examples - think about your travel niche. Write down who might be interested in your articles and then review your list once more to reorder the list into hot prospects. Package your submission before you send it or present it. You know how to package – use colour, use your images… make the person who opens your email (or envelope if that is how you are submitting your work) say WOW! Followed by, "We gotta talk to this writer!"

When sending images online make sure they are very low resolution. If you can protect your image with a watermark, then do so. You can also add a watermark to your documents using MS Word or add a stamp if you are using Adobe Acrobat PDFs. The watermark and stamp should indicate a copyright symbol with your name alongside it. That copyright digital signature should look like this: © 2018 Steve Crowhurst. You can find the copyright symbol by clicking on the Insert a Symbol icon.

Once the table opens up, click on the Symbols tab and you will see the full display. Scroll down until you discover this symbol:

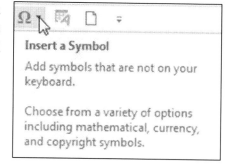

**Insert a Symbol**

Add symbols that are not on your keyboard.

Choose from a variety of options including mathematical, currency, and copyright symbols.

To insert into your Word document, click the Insert Symbol icon. Select the Font and Subsect as you see in the table. Select the copyright symbol, then click Insert. Then click Close. After that, you can highlight the icon and change the font size as required. Job done.

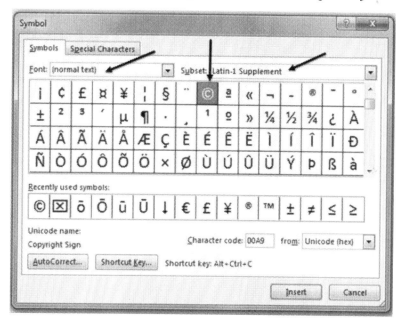

# INVOLVE YOUR AGENCY TEAM & CLIENTS

There may come a time when you need to expand your writing production, especially if you start publishing your own e-magazine. To help you with your writing assignments you might want to consider involving your agency team and also your clients.

As each member of the agency team travel, they should make notes for an article to be written when they return. If they can write and travel at the same time, they could email their latest thoughts and comments on and about where they are at that moment in time. Now that would be fresh content, and that is precisely what your readership wants.

With this level of fresh content flowing to you, you can turn it around and post it on the agency's social media sites and the agency website, too.

If you can determine who, out of your client list is a writer, then you could approach them and ask if they would like to contribute to your publication. Most of the time they would write for free and be satisfied just seeing their name in print. Quite often this is all they need as motivation. It also offers boasting benefits when they connect online with their friends. A client's recommendation also helps you sell more travel.

If you have more than a few clients who like to write and write well, you might suddenly be looking at arranging a group departure. How about the annual writer's festival held at Wye in Wales? Or perhaps a tour of old book shops in major cities around the world – one city even. One more idea – a travel writing workshop held somewhere other than your home city. Go somewhere creative. Inspiring.

If the signs are encouraging, why not hire in a well-known author to accompany the tour group. At each stop, hold a workshop. Publish the group's articles in a special issue of your magazine.

A few things are happening here: you have generated new revenues from this trip, you have acquired a writing team, chances are the group will want to travel to another area of the world to write about it, and you have a source of excellent content for your magazine PLUS what you write. That is not a bad day's work!

## Literary Traveller

If you would like to sell into readymade tours, explore this website – the Literary Traveller. You may be able to sell into their tours and take your travel writing group with you.

http://www.literarytraveler.com/

# USING YOUR WEBSITE AS A HUB

Your website could and should be the HUB for all things related to marketing travel and especially if you are an independent contractor/ homebased agent without an agency window. Your website is where you direct your newly acquired readership.

Depending upon the location of your agency, your agency window will be looked at and glanced at a few times to a few hundred times each day. If you are not facing onto a main street of a major city, or you are home-based, then your website becomes the digital equivalent of an agency window.

When a client or prospect clicks to your webpage, you will want them to be excited about landing there. The visuals they find on your website should be stunning and the text captivating. They should see offers and deals and links to access your articles, your e-magazine, your eBooks and novels.

If this works as intended, your clients will be well read and ready to book. Make visits to your website like peering through the glass of your agency window. They will become enraptured by the exotic places pictured there. Do the same for your social media too.

All roads lead back to your website –
even from your social media sites.

# FROM FAM TO E-PRINTED POSTCARDS

You are away. You are on a FAM. You are cruising the high seas or cruising the beaches. No matter where you are, there is a postcard in a rack, waiting for you to buy, jot a few lines on the back and mail it home. Alternatively, you create a digital postcard, add text, and send to all your clients in a matter of seconds. You might even post this postcard on your Facebook page.

## SnapShotPostcard App

Here's an app that can help. From your smart phone, you arrange for hard copy postcards to be snail mailed to whomever. Where there's one, there's many more. Search for the postcard app that works for you.

http://www.snapshotpostcard.com/solution/

Check this out also. https://sincerely.com/postagram

## Supplier's Postcards

Your suppliers, especially tourist boards and hotels, can offer you both e-cards and hard copy postcards to send. Your choice. However, a physical postcard, with a country stamp on it still has pull. Sent from you saying, "Wish you were here? You could be."

## Oversized and More

There are specialty advertising companies who can print hard copy oversized and custom designed postcards for those special announcements. Watch what your suppliers send you. They use this type of marketing tool when they market to you.

# GO ANIMOTO

Another of my favourite DIY video tools. Animoto is a fantastic easy to learn tool for promoting your latest article, your photography and your latest trending destination. You build your video using images, text and video clips. The basic account is free, and the next level up is only $39 per year. I suggest you splurge and buy the $39 account. Animoto is very easy to learn, and you can create videos on the road using the Animoto app.

Imagine a 60-second commercial to a 3-minute travel video that features a series of images and footage shot by you. Add captions and short sentences to entice the reader. Add one or two ten-second video clips to add voice and movement and all of this unfolding to a sound track of your choice. The last image in your Animoto video is asking the viewer to visit link they see on screen.

Here's a sample Animoto video I put together for you. It is very short but delivers the concept that you can develop and expand on using your own words, video and stills.

Think of all the ways you can use Animoto to spread the word about your travel writing and your latest posts. Once finished, you can embed your Animoto videos into your website and post them on your social media sites too. Even export them to your YouTube channel.

Animoto videos can be edited, updated time and again. It is extremely versatile. Type the bit.ly link into your browser to view my video.

www.animoto.com   http://bit.ly/2p5djlm

# SELLING YOUR PHOTOGRAPHY

The images you capture during your travels will support your travel writing and travel blogging, however, each image by itself, if it is top quality and high resolution, can also generate its own revenue – just for you.

## Here's how you can generate revenue from your photography:

1.  Sell your image to:

    - travel magazines

    - tourist boards

    - online image banks

2.  Upload to stock photo sites like Shutterstock to earn a royalty.

3.  Print your image on canvas, fine art paper to sell from local art galleries or sell online via art and photo publishing services.

4.  Publish as:

    - Book covers

    - DVD covers

    - Screen savers

    - Art posters

    - Postcards

    - T-shirts

To succeed in the world of digital photography you are going to have to measure up to the photographers who work for National Geographic – and that is a tough act to follow if you intend to reach that level. Your photography can generate revenue for you without having to stretch that far. Check the list of possibles above and highlight the ones that interest you.

The market place is wide open to you, and no one can tell you that your photography does not measure up. Your sales will tell you all you need to know. No photography sales – means stick to writing. Keep writing, keep selling travel and use your images to support your articles.

As long as you have an artistic eye, you can take control of this opportunity by turning your image into a poster or fine art print. Once printed or at least created and stored, you can then promote and sell your artwork online, or as a framed hard copy via a local art gallery. Check this website out: www.fineartamerica.com they operate worldwide.

Here's one of my photo-to-art images. Print size is 8.5 x 25 inches.

# IMAGES TO SCREENSAVERS

Screensaver software gives you the opportunity to turn your photographs and videos into screen savers and send them out to your readership and agency travel clients. Annotate your images, so your name is always up front. Your screensavers would be appearing on prime time PC, right about here…

Screensavers can be static or visually stunning. You can add video, QR codes, links and more so that the client looking at your screensaver on their computer screen has instant contact to your articles, website, blog  and any other side of yourself you want to promote.

Most screensaver software programs will instantly load your screensaver to the client's desktop once downloaded. If you want to see this in action, you can download a screensaver from one of your preferred suppliers. Yes, your supplier's have been using screensaver technology to spread their brand for many years now.

Think how you can create and update those screensavers each time you travel and write a new post on your blog. You can also  promote your new screensavers via Facebook and Twitter and in your regular client e-mails too. Here's one screensaver program for you to review. One time cost is USD$39.95.

https://www.blumentals.net/scrfactory/

# BONUS PAGES

# HOW TO PUBLISH YOUR TRAVEL BOOK ON AMAZON.COM

You need to know about this. It's important. You can explore Amazon's CreateSpace self-publishing platform by yourself, however it will help if you know how to navigate them before you view them. The next section will help you navigate those same CreateSpace pages a little faster.

After reading this section, when you do decide to publish your guide book, how-to book or your romance novel, you will be well-informed and eager to finish your book.

Turn the page and carry on!

# WHAT DO YOU WANT TO PUBLISH?

Now there's the question of the day. So many books to write, things to say, knowledge to share – what rises to the top of your list? What is the book you most want to write? Is it a guidebook, a how-to book, a travel romance or adventure novel? So many, perhaps too many, choices. You will need to narrow it down, or, list all the books you would like to write, decide the order in which they should be published and get busy.

Amazon.com is the platform you will publish on, and CreateSpace is Amazon's DIY application where you follow the steps to create an account, get an ISBN number for your book, then follow the clicks all the way to publishing. The first step, however, is to write your book. This guide will help you once you have your manuscript written, edited and ready to go.

If you are not a natural writer, there are courses you can take, and if you wish, you can employ the talents of people who edit books and people who design book covers. The help you need is one click away. Search on-line or use the support services offered by CreateSpace.

Now, back to your manuscript. First things first, get it out of your head and 'on paper' as in typed into a Word document. Do this without any thought about where the commas go. Just get those ideas recorded and saved.

## The Title

The title is very important come the time you want to publish. It is one of the main attractions for a prospective reader looking at the cover of your book on their computer screen. Using CreateSpace, you cannot change the title once it is published.

## The Subtitle

Just as important as the title – the subtitle is the short explanatory one-liner somewhere on that cover page, or just under or close to the title itself. The subtitle text should support, add to the main title.

## The Cover

The cover and the title work hand-in-hand, so the combination has to work graphically and attract the reader to your publication. CreateSpace offers a book cover application where you can create a cover using their templates. For a few hundred dollars, have CreateSpace create the cover for you. Alternatively, seek out a friend who is a graphic artist.

## The ISBN Number

CreateSpace offers a free ISBN number service. Follow the prompts and fill in the form which means listing your book title and subtitle. Once you type in this information the ISBN number is created. Once you click SAVE there is no going back. That ISBN number is attached to your book. You can change the title by requesting CreateSpace support for assistance. Better to get it right the first time.

## Bye, Bye Publisher Rejections

Isn't that a nice thing to know? When you self-publish through CreateSpace there is no one to tell you "no chance, it will never sell" or "yeah, but we don't publish that kinda stuff." The only response you will get from CreateSpace is positive. They want you to succeed. If you turn out a best seller, they will profit – as they should.

It is worthwhile looking at the current top ten novel or guide books. Check the covers, look at the colours, the layout, the titles, fonts, subtitles and so on. In other words, study what is selling. Look at the chapter pages and titles and the intro pages too. There are so many different layout styles already in print. You can learn from them all. Be it a novel, guide book, a photographic book – each one has something to teach you.

You can do this research while you are writing your book. Take a break, head to a book store and start your research. Keep it apples to apples. If you plan to publish a travel guide then review the top selling travel guides. If it is a romance novel then head to that section.

## No Publisher BUT...

With no publisher involved you will be doing all the marketing. CreateSpace has thought of almost everything. They offer tips, tools and expertise. One thing to know is that many of those publishing houses that wouldn't consider publishing your book, scour Amazon.com pages for new titles just in case there is a book they would like to publish. This also happens with movie companies. Everyone is looking for that next million dollar pay day and who knows, it could be your self-published book that attracts them. If that does occur for you then you'll need a lawyer, a literary agent and someone to carry your cash!

## Types and Sizes

Today, it's not necessary to write a 500 page book. You can write a 100 page novella. A short story as it were. Most trade paperbacks are now publishing in the 6" x 9" size. The smaller paperbacks are 5.5" x 7" – check the chart on the CreateSpace website.

## EBooks

Once you've published your paperback book using CreateSpace, it's a couple of clicks to move your manuscript across to the Kindle format and publish it as an eBook.

Note: The CreateSpace Interior Reviewer will not look the same when converted to a MOBI file – the format for Kindle. So, here's what you do: you send your word document to www.word-2-kindle.com. Pricing starts at USD$49. Give the team at word2kindle a week and you'll receive two file formats: Mobi and ePub. Do it right the first time. No stress! Upload the Mobi file to the Kindle page.

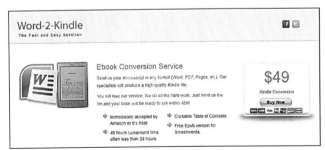

# WHERE DO YOU START?

You can create an account with CreateSpace with or without a manuscript, and I found having an account gave me the nudge each day to fulfil my self-imposed obligation to finish my book.

I am assuming you have a title, a manuscript, an editor, a cover…and more or less your book is ready to go. Ready to be published. Yes? No? If no, no matter. CreateSpace has all the info you need.

## CreateSpace Homepage

Start here - click to www.createspace.com and begin reading. Get familiar with the page and the information. I can tell you if you follow their advice you will succeed in publishing your book. That does not mean it will sell. That is a whole new element called marketing.

As you can see below, you have two choices: DIY or paid services at very reasonable rates. To do it yourself, you may have to call in a few favours from your friends. English teachers to edit, well-read pals to read your proof copy and comment on the flow, story, layout.

## Be sure to read this page in full:

The page image below contains the links you need to explore the CreateSpace tools. You will find this page here at this link: www.createspace/Products/Book. I will be showing some of the tools as we progress. Be sure to read every word and click on every link and follow it through to the end. Once you know how CreateSpace works, your frustration level will drop.

# THE COSTS OF SELF-PUBLISHING & ROYALTIES

The most beautiful thing about self-publishing on CreateSpace is that it is free to use. There are no costs involved unless you hire in their editing and book cover creation services. When you set up your book, you will fill in the blanks regarding the size, the number of pages, then select a glossy or matte finish to your cover. This information allows CreateSpace to determine their printing costs.

## Your Selling Price

Based on your information, CreateSpace calculates their cost. You then add your profit margin, and the combination becomes the price your book will sell for. See below for how this works on the sample royalty calculator. The numbers would change when you complete this page with details of your publication. Your cost per book for when you want to purchase them is very low. The one you are reading now would cost you about USD$3. You can buy as many copies as you need to resell to agency clients, sell at local markets or online.

**Royalty Calculator***

Use the royalty calculator to figure out how much you'll make every time your book is manufactured.

**Print Options**

| Interior Type | Black and White ▾ | Number of Pages | 300 |
| Trim Size | 6" x 9" ▾ | | |

| List Price | | Channel | Royalty |
| --- | --- | --- | --- |
| | | Amazon.com | **$3.32** |
| USD $ 12.95 | Calculate | eStore | **$5.91** |
| | | Expanded Distribution | **$0.73** |
| ☑ Yes, suggest GBP price based on the U.S. price | | Amazon Europe | **£2.21** |
| GBP £ 9.86 | Calculate | For books printed in Great Britain | |
| ☑ Yes, suggest EUR price based on the U.S. price | | Amazon Europe | **€2.28** |
| EUR € 10.80 | Calculate | For books printed in continental Europe | |

I selected the Black and White interior which refers to the text. The size of the publication is 6 x 9, and I have a page count of 300. Then I added the list price that I would want my book to sell for – that is the USD$12.95. Click calculate, and the rest of the form populates.

To the right, on the calculator form, you can see two columns: Channel and Royalty. If someone buys your book from the Amazon.com website, you will earn USD$3.32. Sell 100 books, and you have made USD$332.

NOTE: when you complete this form from within your account it works a little differently because the pricing calculated is based on your input. The cost to Amazon appears first. You then consider their costs, what the market will bear and add your profit/royalty.

**This video plays on the CreateSpace website and YouTube. It informs you about your royalty income.**

https://www.youtube.com/watch?v=1GmHwjt_EUc

# CHEQUE OR DIRECT DEPOSIT?

When you complete the financial / tax form within your CreateSpace account, CreateSpace wants to know if you want your royalties paid by cheque or by direct deposit. Now here's a tip for Canadian authors (if you did not know this, it would take you a while to find out):

1. Direct deposit applies only to American authors. Americans can receive their royalties within days of a book being purchased.

2. There is no direct deposit system for Canada. Canadians can only receive royalties by cheque and only once the royalties reach USD$100. Using the numbers from the royalty calculator, you would have to sell 30 books online before CreateSpace cuts you a cheque.

For the Canucks – there is nothing wrong with the formula and it saves accounting for three-dollars every so often. Note: if you published through a publishing house, your royalty would be a staggering fifty-cents per book sold – or something like that. Now, that would change if your book sold a million copies. Even then, one million x .50 cents… that ain't bad!

**Kindle offers both:**
Referring to non-American authors, Canadian for instance: when you complete the tax information pages on your Kindle account, you can select direct deposit or cheque.

# OPENING AN ACCOUNT

The logical next step is to open an account and as mentioned before, when you do this, even if your book is only half written, you will feel as if you are joining something that will eventually get your book published. You will be committed to finish writing. You will want to see your book cover on the Amazon.com platform. So, fill in the blanks and keep clicking for the prompts. Click to this link when you are ready: www.createspace.com/Signup.jps. Here's what the page looks like.

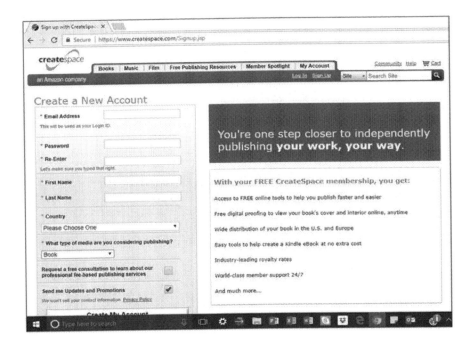

It is that simple, and once you click the Create My Account tab at the bottom, magical worlds unfold – meaning you now have the power to write and publish your very own book. To receive your royalties, you must complete the TAX forms and submit them electronically. They are straight forward, however, to repeat: if you are a Canadian, select CHEQUE versus Direct Deposit – there is no DD for Canada. Canadians use their Social Insurance Number (SIN) where SSN or TIN is shown on the form.

# COMPLETING THE TAX INTERVIEW FORM

The form is straight forward for Americans, with a couple of things to know if you are Canadian.

Here is the top of the form that you will complete online. Read and understand the box opposite the arrow I have inserted. The way it is written is a little confusing as it starts with two negatives one after the other: Do NOT use… if you are NOT… meaning you CAN use this form if **you are completing it as an individual**.

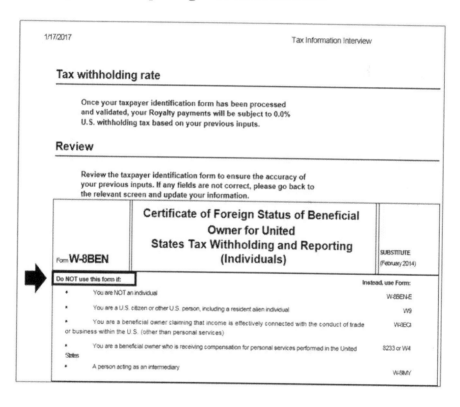

On the next section of the form, see the arrow I have inserted – that is where, if you are Canadian, you type in your Canadian SIN #.

| Identification of Beneficial Owner | |
|---|---|
| **1** Name of individual who is the beneficial owner YOUR NAME | |
| **2** Country of citizenship<br>America or Canada | |
| **3** Permanent residence address (street, apt. or suite no., or rural route). **Do not use a P.O. box or care of address.** | |
| City or town, state or province. Include postal code where appropriate.<br><br>Country | |
| **4** Mailing address (if different from above) | |
| City or town, state or province. Include postal code where appropriate.<br><br>Country | |
| **5** U.S. taxpayer identification number (SSN or ITIN), if required (see Instructions) | |
| **6** Foreign tax identifying number (see instructions)<br>CANADIAN SOCIAL INSUIRANCE NUMBER HERE | |

If you are Canadian, pay attention to item #2: as your previous answers show up here and so it should read for a Canadian - NOT A U.S. PERSON.

Re item #4: Tax Treaty between American and Canada – yes Canada is a "Treaty Country" – you are good to go.

---

Tax Information Interview

**Claim of Tax Treaty Benefits**

9 I certify that the beneficial owner is a resident of Canada within the meaning of the income tax treaty between the United States and that country.

10 **Special rates and conditions** (if applicable—see instructions): The beneficial owner is claiming the provisions of Article XII of the treaty identified on line 9 above to claim a 0.0% rate of withholding on (specify type of income): Royalty.

Explain the reasons the beneficial owner meets the terms of the treaty article

Under penalties of perjury, I declare that I have examined the information on this form and to the best of my knowledge and belief it is true, correct, and complete. I further certify under penalties of perjury that:

1. I am the individual that is the beneficial owner (or am authorized to sign for the individual that is the beneficial owner) of all the income to which this form relates or am using this form to document myself as an individual that is an owner or account holder of a foreign financial institution,
2. The person named on line 1 of this form is not a U.S. person,
3. The income to which this form relates is (a) not effectively connected with the conduct of a trade or business in the United States, (b) effectively connected but is not subject to tax under an income tax treaty, or (c) the partner's share of a partnership's effectively connected income,
4. The person named on line 1 of this form is a resident of the treaty country listed on line 9 of the form (if any) within the meaning of the income Tax treaty between the United States and that country, and
5. For broker transactions or barter exchanges, the beneficial owner is an exempt foreign person as defined in the instructions.

Furthermore, I authorize this form to be provided to any withholding agent that has control, receipt, or custody of the income of which I am the beneficial owner or any withholding agent that can disburse or make payments of the income of which I am the beneficial owner. I agree that I will submit a new form within 30 days if any certification made on this form becomes incorrect.

**Sign Here**

Signature of beneficial owner (or individual authorized to sign for beneficial owner) Date (MM-DD-YYYY)

Capacity in which acting

---

# FILE YOUR BOOK TITLE – GET AN ISBN #

At this stage, you have opened a new account, completed the Tax Interview form online, and printed a copy for your files. Now, when you open your account, you will land on your DASHBOARD, and the important part of this page is shown to the left under a light blue tab: My Account.

Beneath that blue tab, your will see several headings. Be sure to visit each link and read. Note the Message Center – as you progress with your book and complete each stage, you will find CreateSpace keeping you informed by sending you messages to the Message Center.

## Adding the Title of a New Book to Your Member Dashboard

Let's move on to adding the title of your new book. The page shown below is the Member Dashboard home page for your account. You can see headings such as Royalty Balance and lower down, View Detailed Royalty Report – once you have created your title, completed all the steps and your book is published on Amazon – the royalty report is where you check for how many books have sold and the royalty generated.

## Title Information

Here's how you complete the Title Information form. I have left the information on the form that details my next novel – the second in The Sadamune Blades Trilogy. As you look down the form you will see the heading, Series Title. If you are publishing say two or three books in a series, you complete this area. Along that line you will see Volume – meaning the number in the series. This is showing Volume or Book 2 out of the three books I'll be writing. Let's translate that to what you might be writing.

You are going to write a series of travel guides. Let's go for cities: London, Paris, Tokyo and Berlin for instance... okay New York too. So that's a five book series: Volume 1, Volume 2 and so on.

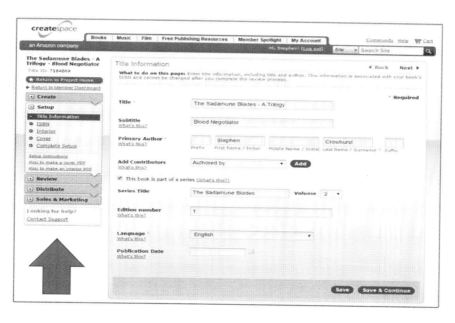

Above this arrow is another menu. This menu keeps you on track as you write your book and move towards publishing it. Some of the steps shown can be completed before you even start writing, or during the writing process. You can secure your ISBN number and you can then type that number into your manuscript, typically page 2 or 3. Check books on your bookshelf to see where the ISBN # is shown. The next heading is INTERIOR – this refers to your complete text.

You review your text using the Interior Reviewer. Make any changes suggested in your Word document, save, review again then re-submit.

Next comes the BOOK COVER. You'll want to try and complete your cover during or after you complete the interior. Finally, you submit your cover and interior text for approval. Wait 2-days and you'll receive a confirmation email. You are almost ready to upload your book to Amazon.com.

## The ISBN Number

If this is your first book, I'm going to suggest you use the tools and services that your CreateSpace account gives you access to – one of them is a free ISBN number. Not only that – you have the support team to answer any questions that arise. There's plenty of information on the CreateSpace site about ISBN numbers plus, as you know, you can Google it and end up reading for the next five years.

Here are the pages related to your ISBN number.

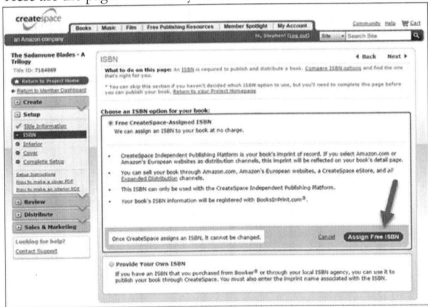

You must click where the arrow is pointing to receive your ISBN#.

# Information on ISBNs from the CreateSpace Website

## What's an ISBN?

An ISBN, or International Standard Book Number, is a unique 10-digit number assigned to every published book. An ISBN identifies a title's binding, edition, and publisher. An EAN, or European Article Number, is a 13-digit number assigned to every book to provide a unique identifier for international distributors. The 10-digit ISBN is converted to a 13-digit EAN by adding a 978 prefix and changing the last digit. We superimpose an ISBN barcode on the back cover (in the lower right corner) of every book we manufacture.

## ISBN Options

When self-publishing your book through CreateSpace, you can use one of our free ISBNs, purchase a Universal ISBN, or use your own ISBN with your book.

## CreateSpace-assigned ISBNs

You may choose to have us assign an ISBN to your book at no charge. All CreateSpace-assigned ISBNs are valid ISBNs purchased from the U.S. ISBN Agency, Bowker.

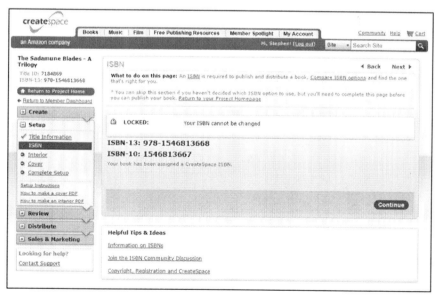

# Important information about CreateSpace-assigned ISBNs

"CreateSpace Independent Publishing Platform" is the imprint of record for all books with a CreateSpace-assigned ISBN.

1. If we assign your book an ISBN, you cannot use the ISBN with another publishing platform.

2. Books with a CreateSpace-assigned ISBN are registered with BooksinPrint.com.

3. A CreateSpace-assigned ISBN is required if you want to sell your book through the Libraries and Academic Institutions sales outlet through the Expanded Distribution.

Universal ISBNs for Purchase

For $99, you can purchase a Universal ISBN using your own imprint through our website via myidentifiers.com.

1. You choose your "imprint of record" for all books with a Universal ISBN.

2. Universal ISBNs can be reused with other publishers if you choose.

3. Universal ISBNs are registered with BooksinPrint.com.

4. You can take advantage of the "CreateSpace Direct" and "Bookstores and Online Retailers" outlets through Expanded Distribution.

To learn more, see the ISBN product page on the CreateSpace site.

I've listed more about the ISBN number from the CS pages, just in case you miss it. Be sure to read everything there is when you return to the CS website.

## Using Your Own ISBN

If you have an ISBN that you obtained directly from Bowker or from your national ISBN agency, you may use it when publishing your book with CreateSpace. If a work has been previously published with this ISBN, the title, author name, and binding type must remain the same. (Binding type refers to a book's format, such as perfect bound, hardcover, spiral bound, eBook, etc. All CreateSpace books are perfect bound.)

During the title setup process, if you use your own ISBN you will also need to enter your imprint, or the name of your publishing company. The ownership and authenticity of all ISBNs are verified.

If you are based in the U.S., you may purchase an ISBN through the U.S. ISBN Agency (Bowker). If you are international, please locate your national ISBN site through the International ISBN Agency. You may also consider registering your ISBN with BooksinPrint.com.

## Copyright, Registration, and CreateSpace
## VERSION 3

Your blood, sweat and tears have gone into creating your book, music or film - now how can you be sure your work is protected through copyright? Copyright is a subject that usually creates many questions among independent authors, filmmakers and musicians. Perhaps one of the reasons copyright is so difficult to fully comprehend is because there is not one answer that works for everyone. Every artist's situation is different, and copyright laws and registrations can be complex. *As a self-published artist, it's up to you to ensure you are protected as you desire.* For that reason, CreateSpace will not register or submit your work for copyright protection under any circumstances.

A basic understanding of copyright is important as you decide what level of copyright protection is right for you. Within the United States, copyright laws are determined by the U.S. government; if you wish to register your work in another country, connect with the applicable government to obtain additional copyright information.

The following frequently asked questions, pulled directly from government sources pertain to U.S. Copyright law:

## What is copyright?

Copyright is a form of protection grounded in the U.S. Constitution and granted by law for original works of authorship fixed in a tangible medium of expression. Copyright covers both published and unpublished works.

## What does copyright protect?

Copyright, a form of intellectual property law, protects original works of authorship including literary, dramatic, musical, and artistic works, such as poetry, novels, movies, songs, computer software, and architecture. Copyright does not protect facts, ideas, systems, or methods of operation, although it may protect the way these things are expressed. See Circular 1, Copyright Basics, section "What Works Are Protected"

## When is my work protected?

Your work is under copyright protection the moment it is created and fixed in a tangible form that it is perceptible either directly or with the aid of a machine or device.

## Do I have to register with your office to be protected?

No. In general, registration is voluntary. Copyright exists from the moment the work is created. You will have to register, however, if you wish to bring a lawsuit for infringement of a U.S. work. See Circular 1, Copyright Basics, section "Copyright Registration".

These four frequently asked questions are just the tip of the iceberg. To learn about copyright and copyright registration, and for the most up to date information, please visit:

http://www.copyright.gov/help/faq/

Shown below is a sample page that you'll find in all books. Notice the layout and the disclaimer at the bottom. Tip re fonts: the Garamond font is widely used in so many books. You are reading it now. For your 6x9 sized book, use a Garamond font size of 12.5.

---

**The Sadamune Blades – A Trilogy**
**Book Two: Blood Negotiator**


© 2017 Stephen Crowhurst
All Rights Reserved


ISBN-13: 978-1546813668
ISBN-10: 1546813667


Cover images from shutterstock.com


Published by Stephen Crowhurst through CreateSpace


Font: Garamond 12.5


Printed in the United States of America


Thank you for buying an authorised copy of this book and for complying with copyright laws by not reproducing, scanning or distributing any part of it in any form without permission. In doing so you support all writers.

*** 

The Sadamune Blades Trilogy, Book Two: Blood Negotiator is a work of fiction and is written to entertain. It should be read as such and nothing more. Names, characters, places, incidents, events, and dates in this novel are either a product of the author's imagination or are used fictitiously. The author has taken some license with historical events to enhance the story. Any resemblance to actual events or locales or persons, living or dead, is entirely coincidental.

---

# SELECTING THE SIZE OF YOUR BOOK

The size of your book is important because it is used to create two templates: one for the interior of your book – i.e. your text. The second for the cover. The size of your book will depend on what type of book it is that you are writing. Do you want it travel size, meaning it will fit into a pocket or purse? Should your book be an eBook so that your travel clients can "carry" it in their Kindle? If you want it noticed, go for the 6" x 9" size. In doing so, you'll have plenty of white space on the cover to fill in with attractive graphics and a title that sizzles.

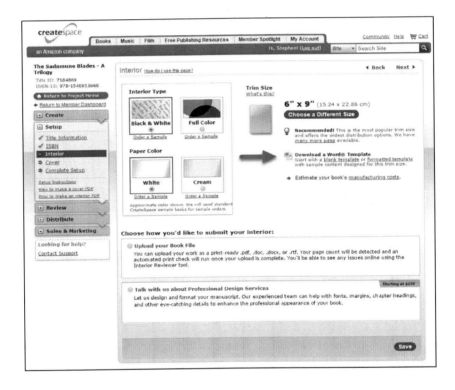

The Interior Template is your text document that you have uploaded to CreateSpace. You can start from scratch and write your book directly into a CS template. You have two choices: You can select a blank template or a formatted one. If you are familiar with setting Sections, Headers, and Footers in Word then you go for the Blank Template. If not – go for the formatted.

## The Cover Template

Check the Black and White interior box for the page count. Select the size of your book and type in the page count. Now if you are typing directly into a formatted template then you will enter the total page count of that template. Be careful if you are typing in a typical letter sized document of 8.5 x 11inches as the page count for that size of document will not be the right count. You must use the page count of the formatted document. Enter that page count and click Build Template.

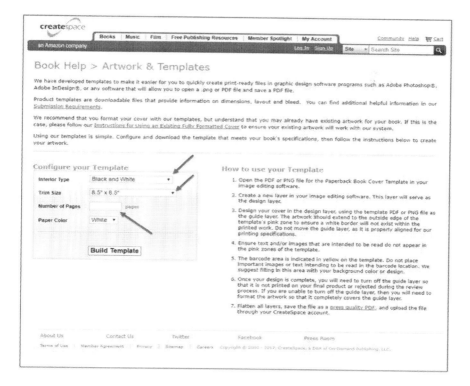

You will receive two cover templates: one PDF, one PNG. It is assumed you are using Photoshop Elements. Right click on the PNG file and OPEN in Photoshop. You will see the layout of the book cover with the dotted lines indicating the trim size. You must be aware of these lines so when your cover is printed you have not cut off any text or part of an image. Hide the PNG template before saving as PDF. Maximum cover file size is 40MB.

# THE INTERIOR REVIEWER

We've arrived at the point where you have written your book and typed or pasted your text into the template that CreateSpace created for you based on the book size you selected. Happy with your edited copy, you now upload your file to CreateSpace. See below: The menu to the right is highlighted in dark blue over the word Interior. Lower down you can see two boxes under the heading: Choose how you'd like to submit your Interior. **Select: Upload your Book file** – that is, if it has been edited by a professional, spellchecked and there are absolutely no errors, PLUS all graphics are at a resolution of 300dpi. If not at 300dpi, you will be advised they may appear fuzzy.

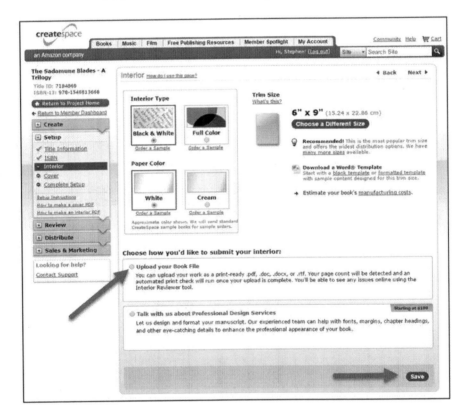

Once submitted, the turnaround time is roughly two full business days. You will receive an email when your files have been reviewed. You might have an error message advising you let's say about a graphic that was not 300dpi or a line of text that runs past the trim line. Another thing to check, and you must check each page in the Reviewer, is to look for any movement of headings, titles and so on. There may have been some hidden formatting in the document you pasted into the Interior Template that the Reviewer cannot read.

These are small but annoying setbacks. To offset these issues make sure the Interior file you upload is in a PDF format. If you upload a WORD document then the formatting issue will raise its head more than once.

Below is what the Interior Reviewer looks like. You can explore this page within the CreateSpace website. As you can see, your text is shown laid out in the reviewer. Any errors are highlighted and you are requested to make amends. Meaning, make the changes in your Word template, save to the PDF format. Save again and resubmit. This means you return to your Dashboard. Click on the title of the book, and half way down the page you will find a link to upload a NEW file. You don't have to rename your file, just upload the same file with the amendments.

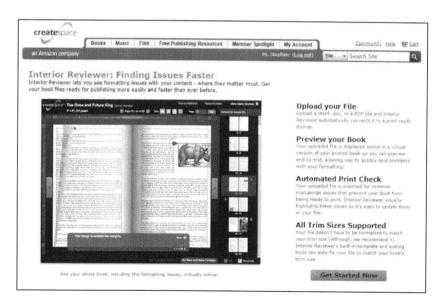

You may make as many changes as you wish, and upload as many times as it takes. Do not rush this. Make sure your book is correct. The worst, the absolute worst is to be so proud of your book, and then you turn to the first line and whoops… a typo! Been there done that! That is devastating. It happens even to well-known authors and even large publishing houses do not catch all the errors. A recent book I read had 12 typos or words missing. Visit the link below for more information.

https://forums.createspace.com/en/community/docs/DOC-1771

Note: Once your book is published and selling on Amazon, and you find a typo, you can still correct the master document, save to PDF and upload the revised file. In doing so your file must go through the usual review procedure. You will wait the same two-days to know the text is accepted. The updated version of your book will be available online soon after – generally in about 5 business days.

## Important: The Interior Reviewer is not working…

The Interior Reviewer does not seem to work on Google Chrome. You can try it and chances are you will be reminded to download the latest Adobe Flash Player. You do that yet still it does not work. From my experience the Interior Reviewer does work on Internet Explorer.

# THE MESSAGE CENTER

Here's how the Message Center looks. Your message alerts will be flagged on your Dashboard home page. Be sure to check each alert and delete when you have completed the task.

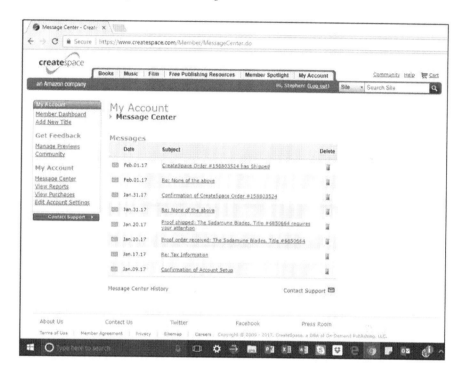

# CREATING YOUR BOOK COVER

There are two ways to do this: DIY or hire in the talent. CreateSpace has a Book Cover Creation Service and the pricing seems to start around $399. Now that is a good price as I know how long it can take to create and also the cost of images if you purchase them. For instance I purchased three stock images from www.Shutterstock.com for my three novels. I paid around USD$48 for the three. Once I had those images I could apply them in any way I wished... meaning use all or parts of them, change the colour or whatever I needed to do to create my cover.

## Travel Covers

It is very likely that if you are writing a travel guide or even a romance novel with a destination / location background scene or theme, then you should be able to request an image from the tourist board for free. Now, this makes for good marketing too. Chances are the tourism board will ask you about the use of their image and if your book will help promote tourism – hey, they might get behind it and help you sell it! That means they might market it, talk about it on their website. That depends of course on the content. If it includes adult content and curse words then they will shy away for obvious reasons. You can always use your own images, and why not. Then there is no cost or legal challenge pending as to who owns the image.

## The Cover Template for a 6 x 9 book with 320 pages

Below is the template CreateSpace built for my first novel Revenge! Your images must meet the edges of the shaded border. The dotted line indicates where the book cover will be trimmed. The grey area on the left hand page is for the Amazon bar code and price.

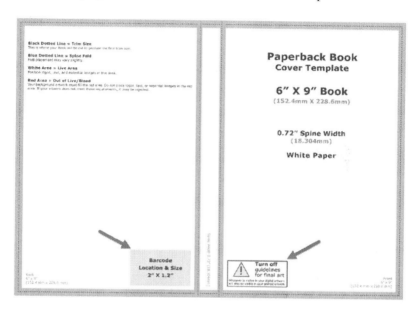

Above: Look at the front page bottom left corner – there is a warning to turn off / hide the PNG template before saving your work in PDF. Below is how my cover looked once completed.

## Using the CreateSpace Cover Template in Photoshop Elements

Here's how the cover of my book looked in Photoshop Elements. There is a lot of work to be done in placing, manipulating, changing colour schemes, selecting text and of course thinking and planning the entire cover strategy. So I have to repeat, if you are not graphically inclined, find someone who is, or use the CreateSpace services.

The cover template shown on the previous page can be seen on the Photoshop dashboard – see the arrow. This is where it sits at the very bottom of the layers. This allows you check where you are placing text and images and to make sure the outer edges of the images are past the dotted lines where the cover will be trimmed. Hide this layer before saving to PDF.

One thing to keep in mind when on a FAM or vacation is to start taking your photographs in Portrait Mode – the reason for this is that the sizing is almost a perfect fit for a book cover. Sure you can crop a landscape shot, but just keep the idea in mind. Also create a folder for Book Cover Images. You never know – you might be publishing more books than you bargained for. Hope so!

# CREATING THE COVER OF YOUR
# TRAVEL GUIDE / LOCATION BASED ROMANCE NOVEL

There are so many options for you to choose from, but it's best to write the book you have always wanted to write, PLUS you could also go for the money and write what travellers are wanting to read. If you are not sure about the answer, ask your clients. That was easy! Here's a selection of book covers found online. Review and decide what type of cover would suit your novel, search images online and see what results you get. For sure, you'll get some new ideas.

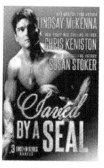

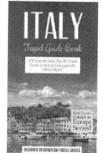

# HOW YOUR NOVEL / TRAVEL GUIDE WILL LOOK

After all your hard work, this is what you will be waiting to see – YOUR book, online at Amazon.com, ready to be ordered, printed and shipped. All at no cost to you!

So now it's time to get busy. Start thinking of the travel guides or novels you want to write, then set yourself a goal and a schedule. The idea here, from my point of view, is that you can make money selling your books, you can use them as giveaways, you can promote with them, and you can also sell them at travel trade fairs and sign them too! Include them when a group departure is booked. You could even develop a group around the theme of your novel. Now there's a plan.

**Come on! Time's a wasting. Let's get busy.**
**Things to do. Books to write!**
**Travel to SELL!**

# MARKETING YOUR BOOK

Your book is just like any other product you sell. It has to be shown, talked about, and mentioned to your clients – just like you do when selling a cruise. If you have let's say 1,000 clients, that's your first list to promote to and guess what? They like travel! Now ask for a referral and if they talk it up to their friends x 2, that's 2,000 to 3,000 more prospects for your book.

CreateSpace has plenty of marketing savvy for you to tap into. You can find the marketing pages by clicking on the Free Publishing Resources tab.

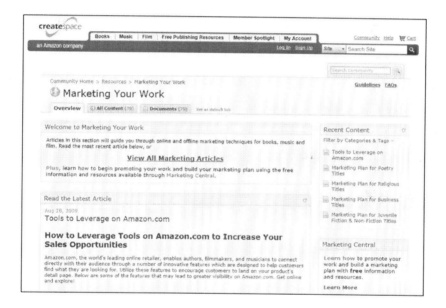

Let's assume your book is in the proof stage – you can order proof copies for about USD$3 to USD$5. Order in ten. Send them to people you trust to read and comment. Send them to magazine editors with a hope they will review and mention.

# "THE ARTICLE OF A THOUSAND WORDS STARTS WITH ONE STEP"

## WRITE YOUR THINGS-TO-DO HERE

What are your next steps to get you started on your Travel Writing Travel Selling journey? What do you have to do personally and professionally to start on this journey? What are the start dates and deadlines? Who is involved? List it all below.

_____

_____

_____

_____

_____

_____

_____

_____

_____

_____

_____

_____

_____

"Either write something worth reading
or do something worth writing."

Benjamin Franklin

# Additional Reference Links

Please note, as with all links, websites come and go. If the link is not live when you click there, search for similar names, companies or services.

http://twournal.com/
http://istw-travel.org/resources.html
http://www.adventuretravelwriter.com/index.html
http://www.burtonholmes.org/life/bio.html
http://www.constantcontact.com
http://www.dummies.com
http://www.journeywoman.com/travel101/tips2004_1.htm
http://www.nuance.com (dragon)
http://www.satw.org/ The Society of American Travel Writers
http://www.shakariconnection.com/women-traveller-books.html
http://www.transitionsabroad.com/listings/travel/travel_writing/travel_writing_general_writing_advice.shtml
http://www.travel-writers-exchange.com/
http://www.women-on-the-road.com/travel-writer.html
http://www.womentravelblog.com/
http://www.writing-world.com/menus/travel.shtml
http://www.writtenroad.com/
https://canadianauthors.org/national/
https://thewritelife.com/interested-in-travel-writing/
https://travelwriting2.com/resources/
https://www.writing.ie/resources/really-useful-links-for-writers-travel-writing/

# About The Author

After a successful career as a travel agent, agency owner, travel trade management consultant, trainer, contributor, publisher, artist, photographer, author and humourous no-fluff no-theory keynote speaker, Steve now focuses on writing travel trade How To books. They are sold by The Travel Institute and Amazon.com.

Steve has been writing How to Sell Travel articles since September 1987 when his first article appeared in PATA TRAVEL NEWS magazine, Americas Edition.

From 2001 - 2016 Steve wrote a monthly sales column for CT Magazine, called Selling With Steve. In addition he wrote How to Sell articles promoting destinations featured in CT.

In 2010 he published a 400 page marketing book for travel agents. In June 2011 he published his own e-Magazines: Selling Travel, IC-Travel Agent and Travel Agency Manager.

In 2017 he published his first novel, Revenge! Book One of The Sadamune Blades Trilogy. In 2018 he published his second novel, Blood Negotiator.

For Steve's complete list of travel trade eGuides, his dedicated website promoting his novels and his photography, please visit the websites shown below.

**eGuides: www.sellingtravel.net**
**Novels: www.stevecrowhurst.com**
**Photography: www.phartography.weebly.com**

# Other publications by Stephen Crowhurst

A Travel Agent's Guide to Ancestry Tours
A Travel Agent's Guide to Attracting & Retaining Corporate Clients
A Travel Agent's Guide to Building an Adventure Travel Niche
A Travel Agent's Guide to Prospecting for New Clients
A Travel Agent's Guide to Weddings & Honeymoons
A Travel Agent's Introduction to Attraction Marketing
A Travel Agent's Introduction to Selling Group Travel
A Travel Agent's Introduction to Women Only Travel
FIT and Group Travel Course Bundle
Handy Clip Art and Graphics That Sell Travel
How to Sell More Books with Do-It-Yourself Marketing
PowerPoint Tips for Travel Trade Professionals
Presentation Skills for Travel Trade Professionals
Selling Faith Based, Spiritual & Personal Journeys
Selling Flexible Independent Travel Arrangements
The Travel Agent's Guide to Charging Fees
The Travel Professional's GO VIDEO! Handbook
The Travel Professional's Guide to Managing Your Career
The Travel Professional's Guide to Selling Travel with Humor
Travel Safety 101 – Expecting the Unexpected
Travel Writing Travel Agents
Using Photography to Sell More Travel
Webinar Presentation Skills for Travel Trade Professionals

## THE POWER OF HOW SERIES
How to Close the Sale
How to Publish on Amazon.com
How to Sell Destinations
How to Sell Travel in Uncertain Times

The above titles are digital downloads in PDF format and can be
read on your eReader, tablet and desktop computer.

**www.sellingtravel.net**

Made in the USA
Middletown, DE
30 August 2018